Presented To:

_____

From:

_____

Date:

_____

life
super-
natural

Lynetta Dent

life
super-
natural

**becoming a
magnet for
opportunity**

DESTINY IMAGE® PUBLISHERS, INC.

P.O. Box 310, Shippensburg, PA 17257-0310

"Speaking to the Purposes of God for This Generation and for the Generations to Come."

This book and all other Destiny Image, Revival Press, MercyPlace, Fresh Bread, Destiny Image Fiction, and Treasure House books are available at Christian bookstores and distributors worldwide.

For a U.S. bookstore nearest you, call 1-800-722-6774.

For more information on foreign distributors, call 717-532-3040.

Reach us on the Internet: www.destinyimage.com.

Trade Paper ISBN 13: 978-0-7684-3857-4

Hardcover ISBN 13: 978-0-7684-3858-1

Large Print ISBN 13: 978-0-7684-3859-8

Ebook ISBN 13: 978-0-7684-8970-5

For Worldwide Distribution, Printed in the U.S.A.

1 2 3 4 5 6 / 14 13 12 11

Dedication

I dedicate this book to my Lord and Savior, Jesus Christ, who paid the price for my freedom. I will serve You radically and passionately all the days of my life.

To my bishop, best friend, faithful lover and husband, Lincoln Dent, who has loved me with an unconditional love. Thank you for being an apostle to our home first. I love you more than you will ever know.

Acknowledgments

My special thanks to Apostle Danny and Yolanda Diaz, Apostle Lenell and Carol Caldwell, Bishop Kenneth and Gloria Fuller, and Apostle John Eckhardt—your wisdom and leadership have catapulted me into new levels of revelation and power.

To my family, friends, and ministry staff—thank you for your continuous prayers and support. I couldn't do this without you.

Endorsements

Life Supernatural blew my mind as I was reading it! There are so many life-changing and life-challenging messages in this book. One phrase in particular that radiates in my mind often is: "Transformational Chamber of the Holy Ghost." My life will never be the same after *Life Supernatural.* I have experienced nothing but life supernatural since meeting this woman of God, and I know that the best is yet to come as God continues to empower His vessel for this appointed time: Apostle Lynetta "Lea" Dent. I personally thank God for the divine meeting of the apostles of this hour. I am truly blessed by knowing them.

Lisa Cole
SWEPT, Inc.

The easiest way to live effortlessly is to learn and understand how to flow in the supernatural. Apostle Lynetta Dent's life expresses this truth clearly and boldly. Her life has been a commitment to Christ, the Holy Spirit, and prayer. It has exemplified that as we remain connected to the Father through the Holy Spirit, nothing will be impossible for us. We can expect this book to truly show us the heart of God.

Dr. Alma Holt
Grace Christian Fellowship Church

Apostles Lincoln and Lynetta Dent are a dynamic apostolic couple with a divine mandate from God to usher the 21st-century believers into divine purpose and destiny.

Apostle Stanley and Janice Rooks
Ram in the Bush Christian Center

Apostle Lynetta Dent's teachings and books are revolutionary. With a paradigm-shifting anointing, this woman of God has taught and imparted into our lives a divine ability to trust and believe God for the impossible. It's life-changing, life-moving, and life-breaking.

Apostle Paul and Willia Anding
Victory Through Christ Jesus Ministries

Contents

Foreword

Life Supernatural is everything that the believer needs to bring balance in his or her Christian life. This book will become a classic in the lives of thousands of purpose-driven people and must be in every library.

Lynetta Dent provides the missing ingredients to know how to bring dreams and fulfillment to pass. The content of this book will make a mark in a person's life that will never be erased.

I learned one thing in life, and that is that principles work for anybody, anywhere, at any time. This is a law that cannot be denied.

So, my sister, thank you for the keys that have brought great success to my life.

—Apostle Lennell and Carol Caldwell
First Baptist World Changers
Detroit, Michigan

Introduction

As citizens of a divine, supernatural Kingdom, we must come to A Place Called Knowing. This is a place where we experience God for ourselves. In the Bible, the word *experience* is synonymous with the word *know*. So to know[1] God, is to experience God. John 8:31-32 in The Message Bible puts it this way:

> Then Jesus turned to the Jews who had claimed to believe in Him. "If you stick with this, living out what I tell you, you are My disciples for sure. Then you will experience for yourselves the truth, and the truth will free you."

I spent many years as a stranger to the covenant, not knowing the truth. I would read about Jesus and all of His wonderful works, but I wasn't experiencing any of them. I would go to bed many nights contemplating leaving the faith simply because not much had changed in my life. I felt I had been lied to by the so-called "happy saints." And in my mind, Christianity had been dramatically overrated.

Although these observations and conclusions were untrue, I still felt like it was hopeless to pursue this invisible God. It was at this point in my life that God Himself stretched out His hand to me and responded to the deep, resounding cry for freedom from the depth of my broken soul.

Placed in what I call the Transformational Chamber of the Holy Ghost, I entered a deliverance process that was designed to bring me from under the grip and power of spiritual and religious bondage. It was here, in this invisible, transformational chamber, where the Holy Spirit began to teach me about different levels of knowing God.

The first was the intellectual level, which is where a lot of believers have stopped—the level that stays in the realm of head knowledge but not heart knowing.

The second was the observational level. At this level you can clearly observe or see something about God.

The third was the experiential level. This is where you experience some things that clearly reflect who God is, and as a result, the experience places a divine imprint upon your heart that you never forget. The imprint is so strong upon your heart and mind that you find yourself defending its reality.

All these levels are important in the process of spiritual growth. But in my life, it has been the experiential level of knowing God that has had the greatest impact. And because of these experiences, I have arrived at A Place Called Knowing. No, this is not some super-spiritual position; it is simply a place where I know that without a shadow of a doubt, He is the only true and living God.

Life Supernatural has been birthed out of 13 years of processing. It is a portrait of my life that expresses in the utmost transparency how God delivered me from poverty consciousness and the demonic grip of religious and spiritual bondage. My ups, downs, mistakes, and victories are clearly laid out so that you can draw out that which you need and apply it directly to your life situation.

For those of you who have been lost in the shadows, *Life Supernatural* will catapult you into a whole new way of living. Like spiritual wings, these writings will take you beyond personal life limitations and into grace dimensions of power and manifestation.

If you're ready, then grab a pen and paper, and let's begin the journey.

Endnote

1. Yada'—Strong's #3045: to know, to perceive, to know by experience, The Old Testament Hebrew Lexicon. In the Bible, there are two Greek words for the words "to know"—*ginosko,* which means "beginning knowledge," and *oida,* which means "intimate, experiential knowledge." *Vine's Expository Dictionary.*

Chapter 1

The Prearranged Path

I'll never forget the voice of the Spirit saying to me, "I've already walked it out for you. I've already been there. So just follow Me."

Ephesians 2:10 in the Amplified Bible reads:

> *For we are God's [own] handiwork (His workmanship), recreated in Christ Jesus, [born anew] that we may do those good works which God predestined (planned beforehand) for us [taking paths which He prepared ahead of time], that we should walk in them [living the good life which He prearranged and made ready for us to live].*

Living a supernatural life will require that we understand that there are spiritual paths that have been divinely orchestrated and prepared ahead of time. This predetermined course of living has been prearranged, predestined, and made ready for us, so that we can experience, enjoy, and live out the good life—or the God kind of life.

The Bible is full of stories about people who found their predetermined course or their prearranged spiritual path to destiny. Abraham, Mary, Gideon, Paul, Saul, David, Joseph, Moses, Jeremiah, and many more were all divinely interrupted and shown the predetermined course and the prearranged spiritual paths of God.

When the angel Gabriel visited Mary in Luke 1, she had no idea that she had been handpicked by God to carry and bring forth the Messiah, our Savior, Jesus Christ. But at the time of revealing, her purpose was unveiled and her prearranged spiritual path was discovered.

Before the angel visited Gideon in Judges 6, Gideon had no idea that he was called to be a deliverer. He was poor and the least in his family. But at the time of revealing, his purpose was unveiled and his prearranged spiritual path was discovered.

In First Samuel 16 God told the prophet Samuel to stop mourning over King Saul. He told the prophet that He had rejected Saul as king and had chosen someone from the house of Jesse to be the new king. That man was David.

David had no idea that he had been chosen to be king. Neither did his father. The Bible says that David was keeping the sheep while Jesse, his father, was allowing his other seven sons to pass before the prophet Samuel in hopes that one of them would be king. But out of all of Jesse's sons, David was the one God had chosen.

None of these occurrences just happened. They were prearranged events that were logged in eternity and at the appointed time were voiced and lived out in the earth realm according to the divine purpose and plan of God.

Don't forget that this predetermined course of living gives us the God kind of life. This is why it is vital that we discover God's predetermined course for our lives both corporately and individually. It is the only course that leads to the good life.

Failure to find this predetermined course will cause us to live as spiritual slaves, in bondage to circumstances. Ephesians 2:2 calls this *"the course of this world."* When we walk according to the course of *this* world and not God's predetermined course, we will spend our lives struggling, toiling, begging, and worrying. We will lead lives that are empty and void of meaning and fulfillment.

Discovering my predetermined course has changed my life. The way I believe is different, the way I think is different, the way I speak is different, the way I move is different, and the way I groove is different. This supernatural transformation has catapulted me beyond personal limitations and into a realm of unlimited possibilities. I no longer live in the *I Can't* zone; for *"I can do all things through Christ [who] strengtheneth me"* (Phil. 4:13). This is my path, my predetermined course, to walk supernaturally manifesting the love, glory, and power of Jesus Christ.

If you are reading this book and desire to know God's predestined plan, His predetermined course for your life, just simply ask Him to show you. Ask and you shall receive (see John 16:24). It is as simple as that. My only admonishment to you is that once He reveals it to you, accept what He shows you and obey what He tells you even in light of yourself or your current situation.

I didn't just wake up one day walking in supernatural power. It's been a long process, and I still don't know everything there is to know. But this is one thing I do know. When you ask God to show you your predetermined course, He will do just that. Not only will He show you, but He will also equip you for "the big picture." The big picture is what He normally shows you first, then you have to walk it out by faith just like Joseph in Genesis 37. Joseph saw his predetermined course long before it manifested naturally; but he had to go through some things that would prepare him for "the big picture" that God had initially shown him in his dreams.

Please remember that God has one plan for your life. That plan, according to Jeremiah 29:11, is to prosper you and not to harm you. It's a plan that will give you hope and a future. So go for it. Ask Him to reveal your predetermined course and watch what happens.

Chapter 2

Messages in the Night

"Tonight as I sleep, the Lord will show me great and mighty things…"

I will never forget a dream I had in 1997. In the dream, I was working as a retail auditor when Jesus showed up at my job. The receptionist came to the back where I was working and told me that Jesus was up front waiting for me. I grabbed my belongings and headed to the front lobby where Jesus was waiting, almost as if I had been expecting Him.

We exited the building and got into a pickup truck. Jesus was the driver and I was the passenger. We ended up on a long, gravel, rocky road. Jesus just kept on driving. Finally we stopped. I noticed that the reason we stopped was because there was a table in the road. We got out of the truck and walked toward the table. We sat down and Jesus began to teach me how to manifest creative miracles.

The first lesson involved cheesecake. Jesus took His hand and stretched it toward the table and, voilà, cheesecake appeared. He stretched His hand toward the table again and the cheesecake disappeared. Then He looked at me and gestured for me to do exactly what He did. So I stretched my hand toward the table and cheesecake appeared. I stretched my hand toward the table again and the cheesecake disappeared. After this, Jesus began to teach me how angels ascended and descended. Then the dream ended.

When I woke up, I knew I had been with Jesus. I also knew that there was a deeper meaning, a deeper message hidden in the symbolism of this dream. But what was it? I mean, why would Jesus visit someone like me? What were the gravel road and the cheesecake all about? Why was Jesus showing me how to manifest creative miracles? What in the world had I tapped into?

A few years passed and the dream of 1997 still made no sense to me. I didn't know of anyone who could interpret my dream, so I just placed it on the shelf—but I never forgot it. Meanwhile, spiritual activity had been turned up in my life since that night in 1997. I started receiving a lot of dreams. These "messages in the night" contained detailed information or what I call "divine intelligence" about myself, my future, my husband, my children, my church, my pastors, and my friends, as well as city officials and national events that would make headline news.

I would dream of laying hands on people and they would get healed. I would see limbs grow out in the spirit. In one dream I walked into an elevator where a man had one leg. A few minutes later the elevator started filling up with smoke. As the elevator filled with smoke, the man's leg grew out right before my eyes.

There would be nights I would be visited by prophets of old. They would share amazing information with me about the Word of God. I remember one prophet visited me and placed two gold stones in my hand. He told me that the two gold stones would stop the enemy from taking from me. He also shared with me that the two gold stones once existed on Earth and were about to be restored.

I would have dreams about money. In one dream, I received information that money was being given away to women, and all I had to do to receive it was to write what I needed on a colored piece of paper. So, in the dream, I wrote everything I needed on the colored piece of paper, and within minutes, the money was in my hand.

When I woke up I ran to Walgreens and followed the instructions of the dream. I found the same colored paper that was in the dream and wrote specifically what I needed on the paper. That same day my husband and I received $1,000 supernaturally. It was the exact amount that I had written on the paper. In other dreams I could clearly see demonic spiritual assignments against people, pastors, and churches. I could also see what strategy to use to thwart their demonic plans. Many times the Lord would identify personal attacks against me, my husband, and our ministry. But He would always provide me with a strategy or a way of escape.

However, one dream in particular shook me up like no other. On September 9, 2001, I received a "message in the night" regarding a vicious attack. In the dream, God used me and my children.

Here is what I dreamt: We were at home when, all of a sudden, intruders were at our back door. These men were Arabian, black, and white. They came through the back door forcefully. I grabbed the kids and we ran across the street to my neighbor's house. When I got inside I ran to the phone and looked out the window to see what the men were doing. I picked up the phone and dialed 9-1-1, but the lines were all busy. As I continued to watch the men from across the street I saw them get into two cars; one was a Saab and the other was a Ford Mustang. They drove the cars around the back of my house. I thought they were gone. But a few moments later I saw them coming toward my neighbor's house. I hysterically told everyone to get in the back bedroom and hide. The men entered the house looking for us. One of them came into the room. I had a machete in my hand and threw it at the man. The man died instantly. The last thing I remember in the dream was a voice that said, "You're going to regret you killed him. Do you know who his brother is?" Then the dream ended.

Don't forget that I received this dream on September 9, 2001. I shared the dream with my husband, my mother, and my pastor. Two days later on September 11 (9/11), my mom burst into my room hysterically and told me to turn on the television. After that she uttered these words, "Your dream has come to pass!"

I sat there for a moment in utter shock. I wondered why God would give me a dream of this sort and not show me what to do as He had done so many other times. It just didn't make any sense to me.

From that moment on, my husband, my mother, and those around me began to listen when I would share with them these "messages in the night." But they weren't the only ones who started listening; I started listening and taking these "messages in the night" a little more seriously than I had before. I bought every book I could on dreams and dream interpretation. I prayed and asked God to help me to understand and interpret what He was saying to me in the night season. I also asked Him to help me understand and interpret the dreams of others.

It was at this point that God revealed to me the meaning of the dream of 1997. This message in the night had actually revealed the calling God had placed upon my life. It was a supernatural call. The gravel road represented the way in which God would bring me into the fullness of this call. It would be sort of rocky, bumpy, and rough at first, but as I gained wisdom, knowledge, and understanding, I would be able to manifest creative miracles through the power of Jesus Christ. There would be no need to worry because Jesus would be driving or leading.

The table represented nourishment, friendship, and unity. It was at this place that Jesus would teach me how to manifest creative miracles. This was a place of relationship and fellowship. The power would flow out of relationship and not formula.

He used cheesecake in my dream because cheese-cake is my favorite dessert. It represented that which I desired and enjoyed. And He knew that I would absolutely enjoy the ministry call that He had placed upon my life.

The key in the dream to walking in this super-natural power would be to do what Jesus did. In other words, follow His lead and His pattern only. Imitate Him. Obey His instructions. As I "followed the Leader," He would use me to manifest His breakthroughs, deliverances, and creative miracles.

Thirteen years have passed since I had that dream in 1997. And let me tell you the road has been rough just like the dream said it would be. But the road has been rough because processing is never easy. That road is now what I call the "Transformational Chamber of the Holy Ghost." It was in this place that I had to learn the ins and the outs of how God works and how God wanted to work in my life personally. I still don't know everything. But the lessons I've learned over these past 13 years have changed my beliefs, my mind, and my life. I can truly say that I am not the same woman I was 13 years ago. I have been completely transformed.

Thirteen years ago I was a miserable Christian woman with no clear purpose or direction in my life. Thirteen years ago I didn't know how to change my circumstances through the power of faith. Thirteen years ago I couldn't recognize the voice of God. Thirteen years ago I didn't know how to pray effectively. I didn't know how to sow and receive God's harvest. Thirteen years ago I was a miserable Christian woman lacking the necessary knowledge and spiritual skill to change my life. But praise God for the "Transformational Chamber of the Holy Ghost"!

Yes, it was tough; yes, there were many tears; and yes, there were many mistakes. But I will tell you: I wouldn't trade that process for anything. Because of the things I had to walk out by faith, today I am a better wife, I am a better mother, I am a better preacher, I am a better leader, and I am a better servant in the Kingdom of God; but most importantly I am a better person.

God has used His written Word, the voice of the Holy Spirit, and dreams as channels to communicate His purposes and plans to me. There was never a time in 13 years when He did not communicate what His intentions were for me. Now there were times I didn't understand what He was communicating to me, and there were times I didn't obey what He was instructing me to do. But nevertheless, the communication channels were left open so I could hear what the Spirit of the Lord was saying.

Oliver Wendell Holmes said it best. Now I don't know if he was a Christian, but I would like to share with you a powerful truth that he quoted: "One's mind, once stretched by a new idea, never regains its original dimensions."[1] This is so true. Because once God opened up the dream realm to me, I never again entertained the idea that God doesn't speak through dreams.

The Book of Job in The Message Bible says:

But let me tell you, Job, you're wrong, dead wrong! God is far greater than any human. So how dare you haul Him into court, and then complain that He won't answer your charges? God always answers, one way or another, even when people don't recognize His presence. In a dream, for instance, a vision at night, when men and women are deep in sleep, fast asleep in their beds—God opens their ears and impresses them with warnings to turn them back from something bad they're planning, from some reckless choice, and keep them from an early grave, from the river of no return (Job 33:12-18).

In this text we can clearly see that God does speak through dreams. The problem is that we don't recognize His presence in these dreams.

Dreams have always been a channel in which divine intelligence has been communicated. Although not the only venue used to reveal divine purposes and plans, throughout the Bible dreams were the primary way that God communicated to humankind. Joseph, Jacob, Pharaoh, Solomon, and Daniel all received messages in the night via the channel of dreams.

Scientists have proven that everyone dreams at least one to two hours every night during a certain period of sleep known as alpha level or light sleep.[2] This is when an individual begins to experience what is called REM sleep or Rapid Eye Movement. At this level of sleep, the eyes of the dreamer begin to move very rapidly. The eyes are moving very rapidly because the dreamer is actually watching what looks like a movie. He or she is observing different scenes in a dream.

It's amazing to me that scientists can prove the existence of dreams, yet many believers have discarded the true power of dreams. This is primarily due to their lack of knowledge and understanding in this area. And this is why I strongly urge pastors to teach more on dreams and the spirit realm.

Over the years, I've heard blood-bought believers say things like: "Oh, I ate too much pizza so I know that dream didn't mean anything"; or, "Girl, God speaks only through His Word and not through dreams"; or even, "My sister, dreams are not for today."

There's an old saying: "Ignorance will cost you." And I've come to see the truth and validity of this saying. If I had listened to those statements, I wouldn't be fulfilling my divine purpose today. If I had listened to those dumb statements, my ministry would have been destroyed by a witch. God revealed that a witch was working against our family and our ministry. This was revealed to me through a dream. And praise be to God who showed us how to fight from the heavenly realm and win!

God used a dream to paint a clear picture of what would happen on 9/11, two days before it happened. Although I didn't know what to do at the time, it still proves that God opens up the spirit realm and allows us to see the future. God used a dream and revealed a healing strategy to me. He used a dream to communicate to me the calling that He had placed upon my life. God used a dream and unveiled to me what was going on in a local pastor's life. As a result, this brother was delivered and is still preaching the Gospel. God has used dreams numerous times in my life to tell me where my financial harvest was. Shall I go on?

Listen, I'm not saying that life should be governed by dreams. I don't live by dreams. I live by the proceeding Word of the Lord. But if God chooses to send His Word to me via a dream, so be it. If it comes through a cat, so be it. As long as the Source is God and the information is based upon His Word, I have nothing to worry about.

We must remember that in the world of dreams, many times the communication is not obvious. Therefore the dream may require interpretation. So never make a hasty move solely based upon a dream. Even if the dream is from the Lord, make sure that it has been interpreted properly.

When I have dreams where the communication is not clear, I seek the counsel of the Holy Ghost, the Word of God, and my husband. There have been times when we have taken the dream to our spiritual father, and he would give us even more insight into what God was saying. Following these simple steps of order will save you a lot of headaches and keep you from a lot of setbacks. Trust me, I know!

I have seen havoc break out in churches due to an unskilled dreamer and their lack of knowledge in dream interpretation. In one incident, a young lady had a dream about her pastor. Well, she immediately began telling everyone in the congregation that something bad was getting ready to happen. She stirred up a real mess in that local congregation because of her assumptions, not a God-given interpretation. In the end, the dream was about her and not the pastor.

Please remember that even when a dream does come from the Lord, there is a proper way to approach the matter. For instance, if you have a dream about your leadership or your spouse, you don't run to them and say, "Hey, I've had a dream about you! I need to talk to you now! I am a prophet, and you need to hear what thus said the Lord!"

Don't be foolish! Calm down and first take the matter to the Lord and make sure your assessment is correct. Then, with the spirit of humility and honor, approach your leadership. Explain to them what you saw in the dream. If they are good leaders and have any type of discernment, they will know what to do. Even if they don't know at the time, good leaders will seek God for clarity on the dream.

Another mistake you can make as a dreamer is to assume that all dreams come from God. This is not true. I don't care how gifted and how anointed you are; always check the source of your dream. A skilled Kingdom dreamer knows that not all dreams are from God. They also know that there are basically three sources from which dreams flow:

- God
- your soul/heart
- the devil

Jeremiah 23:16 (NKJV) says, *"Do not listen to the words of the prophets who prophesy to you. They make you worthless; they speak a **vision of their own heart** not out of the mouth of the Lord."* These types of dreams derive from a wicked heart. Jesus said in Matthew 15:19 that evil thoughts come from the heart of man. And just as an evil thought can flow out of an evil heart, so can an evil dream flow out of an evil heart.

Also remember that many of the dreams you receive are about you. It's true. I know that we would like to believe that many of the gruesome details we see in our dreams are about Sister Sally and Brother Joe. But in the world of dreams many of the messages you will receive will be about you. God will use people and things that are familiar to you. He will also use character traits of these people to actually describe deep things about you.

Dreams oftentimes serve as mirrors reflecting the truth about what's really going on at a deeper level. This can be a real blessing when you understand that God isn't trying to hurt you. He's actually trying to bless you or get something to you.

To do this, many times He requires us to take inventory and examine our own hearts. Christians often spend a lot of time observing the faults of others. As a result, we remain blind to the issues that are really brewing in our own hearts, and no Kingdom growth is experienced. Pruning is part of God's blessing process.

I could go on and on about dreams and the *messages in the night* that we receive. But the purpose of this chapter is not to do a whole exposition on dreams and interpretations. I have material that you can order that will help you in this area. There are also other anointed writers who teach on the subject of dreams, such as Jane Hamon[3] and Ira Milligan.[4] My purpose is to drive out erroneous concepts about dreams and messages in the night and replace these incorrect concepts with the truths that are found in God's Word and in my own life experiences.

So if you're ready to experience something far greater than what you are experiencing on a day-to-day basis, then get your journal and get your pen. Set these items by your bedside and prepare to receive messages in the night. I promise you that life as you've known it will dramatically change. This is simply because Kingdom living is the solution for a boring life.

In your journal, write down questions that you would like God to answer. Just don't be shocked when He answers.

Endnotes

1. "Oliver Wendell Holmes Quotes," brainyquote. com, http://www.brainyquote.com/quotes/authors/o/oliver_wendell_holmes_3.html (accessed December 3, 2010).

2. Mark and Patti Virkler, Hear God Through Your Dreams (Communion With God Ministries; http://www.cwgministries.org/5-How-to-Receive-Gods-Counsel-Through-Dreams.htm).

3. Jane Hamon, *Dreams and Visions* (Ventura, CA: Regal Books, 2000).

4. Ira Milligan, *Understanding the Dreams You Dream* (Shippensburg, PA: Destiny Image Publishers, 2010).

Chapter 3

Enemy to Supernatural Living

There is great disparity in the Christian community between that which we profess and that which we actually do. This is because a war is raging on the inside of us. It's a war between good and evil, light and darkness; a war between the Spirit and the flesh.

As believers it is vital that we gain a better understanding of the flesh and how to walk in victory over it, for it is an enemy to Spirit-led, supernatural living. Serving as a gateway, the flesh is the central control center of demonic activity that uses our thought life as an entry point. Therefore, if we are going to walk in any level of supernatural success, we will have to make a choice: either we will live by the influence of the Holy Spirit and experience all that God has promised, or we will live by the dictates and influences of the flesh and spend our lives void of purpose, power, and fulfillment.

> *For the flesh sets its desire against the Spirit, and the Spirit against the flesh; for these are in opposition to one another, so that you may not do the things that you please* (Galatians 5:17 NASB).

> *Because the carnal mind is enmity against God: for it is not subject to the law of God, neither indeed can be. So then they that are in the flesh cannot please God* (Romans 8:7-8).

I said earlier that there is a war raging inside of us every day. This war is between the Spirit and the flesh. I call this war a "thought war" or a war between two ways of doing things. And guess where this war is fought? This "thought war" is fought on the battlefield of our minds.

My mind is a battlefield where "thought wars" are fought. It's like a boxing ring. There are two fighters: the Spirit and the flesh. Who wins is determined by me, the thinker. For that which I allow is that which will be. And whoever rules my thinking rules my life.

Jesus—through His death, burial, and resurrection—defeated satan, thus liberating us from bondage. So the real battle has already been won. The problem is that many times we Christians don't believe this. And guess what? Satan knows it. So he launches thought attacks against us by constantly bombarding our minds with thoughts that are void of faith and contrary or conflicting with what the Word of God says.

For example, you are believing God for the healing of your child. You know that the Word of God promises you healing (see Ps. 107:20; Matt. 15:21-28). You're standing in faith when all of a sudden you receive a demonic transmission from the dark kingdom that says: "Your child will never be healed. Use some wisdom and stop believing this crap. You've been through enough as it is, and you really need some rest from all of this faith stuff. By the way, it has been five years and your child is still not healed."

Let's look at another example. You have a desire to get out of debt. You've gathered all your bills together, you've devised a strategy, and you've made up your mind that this will be the year you will come out of debt. Well, out of nowhere you receive a demonic transmission, a thought that says: "Why are you doing this? You can't get out of debt. Don't you know the economy is bad right now? You need to use wisdom and wait for the right time. And why are you still sowing financial seeds...don't you think right now with the way things are that you need to be keeping everything for yourself? What if every-thing plummets, then what will you have to fall back on? You really need to think about this. Don't you let those ministers trick you! You remember what happened the last time."

Let me give you one last example. You are single and desire a mate. But you've decided to wait and allow God to bring the right one in the right time. On top of that you've been abstaining from sex. Well, out of nowhere a thought comes to you: "You know you really are doing great. You're going to church, serving the Kingdom of God. But don't you think it's time to think about your desires and your wants? You've been sex free for five years, so why don't you reward yourself? Have a little sex…you know you want to. Don't worry, God will forgive you. I'm just saying make time for you! Sex was created by God for you to enjoy, and you certainly deserve it."

As you can see, the flesh is very crafty in its approach. Did you notice how it used thoughts to stir up ungodly passions and desires? Did you notice how skillfully the flesh shifted the individual's focus from God to self? This is because the flesh has one goal: to move you from under the influence of God, His Word, and the Holy Spirit.

This is why the flesh must be crucified, annihi-lated, and put to death. As a born-again believer you must put a stop to its operation in your life. Remember, the flesh is not your friend. The flesh is your enemy. And if you have any plans of walking in supernatural power and manifestation, you will have to put an end to the operation of this demonic force.

I spent many years living as a low-class, flesh-driven coward! The reason I call it low class is simply because walking in the flesh is low-class living. The flesh is beneath me and should be subservient to me. But due to my mindset and that which I believed, I functioned way beneath my Kingdom privileges. My every decision was fear based. There was no drop of faith in operation. Financially I trusted in people, financial institutions, and credit cards. Rarely did I use the principle of sowing finances to reap finances. When the bills were due, I would become fearful. The flesh would then kick in, transmitting thoughts to my mind such as, "Call your mama and get the money. Go down to the cash advance store and just borrow the money. Or better yet overdraw your bank account and get the money that way. You know it allows you to take out up to $300 more than what's available." Next, I found myself doing exactly what the thought suggested I should do. The result? Absolute bondage!

When we choose to walk in the flesh, the only manifestation we will ever see is bondage. Yes, you can experience temporary relief. Yes, the flesh can even give you a false sense of security. But in the end, the result will always be bondage.

Galatians 5:19-21 proves this:

Now, the works of the flesh are manifest, which are these; adultery, fornication, uncleanness, lasciviousness, idolatry, witchcraft, hatred, variance, emulations, wrath, strife, seditions, heresies, envyings, murders, drunkenness, revelings, and such like: of the which I tell you before, as I have also told you in time past, that they which do such things shall not inherit the kingdom of God.

Now, let's look at this same Scripture in The Message Bible:

It is obvious what kind of life develops out of trying to get your own way all the time: repetitive, loveless, cheap sex; a stinking accumulation of mental and emotional garbage; frenzied and joyless grabs for happiness; trinket gods; magic-show religion; paranoid loneliness; cutthroat competition; all-consuming- yet-never-satisfied wants; a brutal temper; an impotence to love or be loved; divided homes and divided lives; small-minded and lopsided pursuits; the vicious habit of depersonalizing everyone into a rival; uncontrolled and uncontrollable addictions; ugly parodies of community. I could go on. This isn't the first time I have warned you, you know. If you use your freedom this way, you will not inherit God's kingdom.

From these Scripture verses we can clearly see that the flesh is only capable of producing a life of bondage. And bondage is produced by a wrong way of believing, thinking, and speaking. Bondage is defined as the state of being under the control of a force, influence, or abstract power. And sadly, many believers are in this state—not because they have to be, but because in some cases they choose to be.

I am going to say it one more time: the flesh is an enemy to Spirit-led, supernatural living. And if you have any plans of succeeding in the Kingdom of God, then you must crucify the flesh or put to death thoughts and imaginations that do not agree with God's Word!

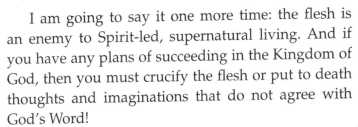

(For the weapons of our warfare are not carnal, but mighty through God to the pulling down of strongholds;) casting down imaginations, and every high thing that exalteth itself against the knowledge of God, and bringing into captivity every thought to the obedience of Christ (2 Corinthians 10:4-5).

This Scripture simply means: do not allow demonic thoughts or strongholds to have rule over you or hold you captive. When thoughts come to your mind that do not agree with God's Word, cast them down quickly! A quick faith response will stop these demonic thoughts from becoming strongholds. A stronghold is simply a demonic, incorrect pattern of thinking. If you allow incorrect thinking patterns to go unchecked, you will find yourself eventually in bondage; because, remember, the only thing the flesh can produce is bondage.

Chapter 4

Solution to Chaos

Chaos is "a state of utter confusion," according to Merriam-Webster's Collegiate Dictionary. It is deviation from order. When one deviates or turns away from the divine law of order, he or she is brought under or subjected to the rule of chaos.

There have been times in my life when I have reaped a harvest of chaos because I chose to deviate from God's law of divine order or God's way of doing things. My husband and I would enter what I call divine flows of manifestation and within months we would find ourselves in a chaotic mess! Now there were times when these demonic seasons of trial were designed to try our faith and were orchestrated by

God. There were other times when these demonic seasons were a direct result of someone putting a "spiritual hit" out on us.

A spiritual hit is when someone sends a spirit of witchcraft against you to stop your Kingdom advancement. They try to accomplish this by speaking word curses over you, your marriage, your family, your ministry, your finances, etc. But not every attack is the result of someone else's doing. We must be prayerful in these seasons and discern what's really going on behind the scenes, remembering that even if God didn't send it, He can still use it.

In our case, there were seasons when we opened the door to the spirit of chaos and confusion. One example in particular, which I will describe in greater detail in another chapter, was when a spirit of oppression came and paid me a visit at my home. I'll never forget sitting at my dining room table with tears rolling down my face. I felt like the weight of the world was on me and I couldn't see any way out. The bills were due, my children needed things, my husband and I needed things, but we didn't have enough money to take care of any of it. I looked up, but no words would come out of my mouth. My tears were liquid prayers and were the only thing I could communicate at that grievous moment in my life.

It was at this moment that a God thought came to me, and with this thought came a righteous indignation. A warlike nature rose up in me and I ran to my bedroom. I grabbed my purse and pulled out my wallet. I only had a few dollars in it, but it didn't matter. I took those few dollars and ran back into my dining room and did something rather strange: I opened my mouth and said, "You foul demon of oppression, I command you to *GO*, now, in the name of Jesus. And here's a seed to show you that I mean business!"

I sat there for a moment looking like a madwoman, but then something amazing happened. A peace filled the room. A power so thick and tangible penetrated the atmosphere of my home. I knew that God was there and the demon of oppression had left the building. Light invaded the darkness and life came.

Over the next few days we experienced an open Heaven over our lives. We saw tremendous financial increase. We were able to give to the Lord, pay our bills, bless our children, bless each other, and bless others. We even had some left over.

Please hear me. This manifestation was a direct result of aligning with the Word of God. Don't forget that God's Word is God's order and is the solution for chaos. In this case God was allowing me to clearly see that when dealing with financial oppressive powers, the giving of sacrificial financial seeds in faith would annihilate, stop, cut off, and sever this spirit's operation in my life. He wanted me to see it and He wanted me to incorporate this principle, this power key, into my lifestyle. It was not to be used just one time. It was a spiritual principle, therefore a weapon that could be used over and over and over again against the force of financial oppression.

Any deviation from order will result in chaos. When people deviate from a truth, they forsake it or turn and go another way. And that's exactly what my husband and I did. We deviated from the order of God. We forsook the path, the way, the divine order that God had laid out for us by not continuing to sow sacrificial financial seeds in the face of financial opposition. As a result, we found ourselves back in the same situation again.

A short time later we were revisited by this demonic spirit of oppression. I would like to say that we kicked its tail by speaking the Word of God and sowing a financial seed just as we had done before, but that's not what happened. Instead we found ourselves under the grip of this spirit again. We did what the Bible refers to as *poroo* in Mark 6:52 (the word "hardened" in English). We lost the power of our understanding and the mental power to go forward.

It was like a stupid demon had gotten hold of me. You would have thought God had never told me anything! There I sat, weighted down, pressed under, heavy, not able to rise, bent over, and stuck! And the sad part is, I did nothing about it. As a result, we went backward and not forward. Jeremiah 7:24 says, *"But they hearkened not, nor inclined their ear, but walked in the counsels and in the imagination of their evil heart, and went backward, and not forward."*

Demonic activity increased in our lives as a result of our unwillingness to continue in the truth that God revealed. Matthew 12:43-45 in The Message Bible tells us:

*When a defiling evil spirit is expelled from someone, it drifts along through the desert looking for an oasis, some unsuspecting soul it can bedevil. When it doesn't find anyone, it says, "I'll go back to my old haunt." On return it finds the person spotlessly clean, but vacant. It then runs out and rounds up seven other spirits more evil than itself and they all move in, whooping it up. That person ends up far worse off than if he'd never gotten cleaned up in the first place. That's what this generation is like: You may think you have cleaned out the junk from your lives and gotten ready for God, **but you weren't hospitable to My kingdom message, and now all the devils are moving back in.***

See, God's Word is God's order. And God's Word must not be forsaken or deviated from. For any deviation from truth is error. And where error is, you will always find chaos and confusion. My husband and I erred when we forsook the way in which God was calling us to live. This way or this divine order of living was revealed to us by revelation. God's desire for us was to walk in supernatural power and provision. In other words, we would have to possess by faith everything we needed and desired. Every time we tried to live by any other means, God would announce His displeasure by removing the power current we were flowing in.

No, He didn't leave us or forsake us, but He made it very clear what He expected from us and how He wanted us to live. This was His Word over our lives; therefore this was His order or His customized design for Lincoln and Lynetta "Lea" Dent. And He expected us to walk in this revelation, live by this revelation, and not deviate from this revelation.

Today, things are different. My husband and I are walking and living in God's flow of divine order. This doesn't mean that every "i" is dotted and every "t" is crossed in our lives, for we make mistakes just like anyone else. But I will tell you this: life for us has changed, and I mean really changed. We are absolutely enjoying obeying God; and as a result, chaos has no rule over our lives.

This of course doesn't mean that we don't go through things, for the Bible tells us that as long as we live in this world there will be trials and tribulations (see John 16:33). We can't get around it. But what we can do is handle it the way God's Word says to handle it and flow in His divine order. As we do this, joy, peace, clarity, fulfillment, prosperity, long life, happiness, and wholeness will be the harvest that we reap.

Chapter 5

I Serve God With My Spirit

"Today I rise with new confidence and fresh revelation. I am a spirit being."

It is impossible to walk in the fullness of supernatural power without understanding that God is a Spirit, we are spirit beings, and the role that the Holy Spirit plays in all of this. In my opinion, it is one of the reasons that many believers are not experiencing the life that the Word of God promises. Of course there are other factors involved, but in this chapter I would like to specifically address being a spirit being who works in conjunction with the Holy Spirit.

For years my life as a Christian was a living nightmare! I had no peace, no joy, no fulfillment, and no clear directions and instructions. I was a broken soul desperately needing something, longing for something, and desiring something. The only problem was that I didn't know what that "something" was. I didn't know what I was looking for. For I had not seen it modeled before me.

Finally, after much mental toiling, I came to this conclusion: Christianity is powerless and incapable of changing my life. Although it was the wrong conclusion, it seemed like the only logical explanation at the time. For if one hears of power but never experiences that power, what good does it serve?

See, events in life have a way of bringing us to these conclusions. A conclusion is defined as an ending or a stopping point. It's a place where a decision is made and the mind is made up about something. And because of the events that had transpired in my life, I drew the line of finality and mentally decided that the "church thing" didn't work. There was no convincing evidence that this God was real, at least not that I knew of.

I don't know if you know this, but God likes to flex. He loves to take nonbelievers and make believers out of them. He loves to take what looks impossible and make it possible. One of the ways God accomplishes this is through giving a person what I call a "God Experience." A God Experience is not limited to one isolated event. For some it can be a series of encounters with the Divine. These encounters with God are designed to liberate you from hazardous materials and bring you into the full knowledge and understanding of Kingdom realities and truths.

The hazardous materials I am referring to are our traditions, perspectives, and beliefs that are not God-centered. Hazardous traditions, perspectives, and beliefs pose a level of threat to our lives, our health, our prosperity, our peace, our abundance, and our overall sense of well-being. This is simply because they are not God-centered.

As I mentioned previously, I have spent the past 13 years in what I call the Transformational Chamber of the Holy Ghost. It has been in this place that God has used love, fire, grace, mercy, and of course the Holy Spirit to remove hazardous traditions, perspectives, and beliefs from my life. This process, although it was very painful at times, has produced in my life a fresh, radical approach to living. I have a different outlook on life. For I see now from an eternal perspective, not ignoring the physical, just knowing that I have power over it. I now know that I am a speaking spirit being who has been created in the very image and likeness of my Father who is God.

Yes, I live in a body and I have a soul. But I am not controlled nor limited by either one. For I serve God with my spirit, allowing the Holy Spirit to influence my every word, my every thought, and my every action.

Apostle Paul tells us in Romans 1:9 that we serve God with our spirit. Our spirit is the main control center of supernatural activity. It is where God's Spirit, the Holy Spirit, is housed. This means that inside the real you, who is spirit, resides God Himself. Everything He is and has is available to you as a born-again believer and flows out of this place. All you have to do is believe this truth and allow the G-life (the God kind of life) to flow out of the real you, which is spirit. This is what we call "living out of your spirit."

When we gave our lives to Jesus Christ, the Holy Spirit joined with our spirit. So "living out of our spirit" is equivalent to living and walking in the Spirit. It simply means that we are allowing the Holy Spirit to influence every part of our being. This includes our thoughts, our words, and our actions.

"Living out of your spirit" can be quite rewarding. Let me give you a personal example. One day I was driving when all of a sudden a thought flashed across my mind. I ignored it at first. A few moments later the Holy Spirit spoke to me and told me to prepare a conference. He gave me very specific details about the conference: the size of the room, what He wanted my husband and me to teach, and how much to charge. However, this was at a very trying time in our lives. We were just coming out of a horrible storm and only had one vehicle. Yes, we owned it, but with children and work schedules we needed two cars.

Well, God knew that. So through His Spirit He communicated to us what to do to reap what we needed. All we had to do was obey the instruction or *live out of our spirit*—which is what we did. Then, as a result of choosing to obey that instruction, we reaped a debt-free Lexus at the meeting. There was no toiling, no running from car lot to car lot begging finance companies to approve us. It was just a matter of timing and responding to the voice of the Holy Spirit.

As I said earlier, our spirit is the main control center of supernatural activity. So if you're looking for some action, make sure you're looking in the right place—inside you—because the real action is in your spirit. I mean, come on, God is there! And have you ever known a dull moment with God? Well, I haven't. And contrary to many teachings, the Kingdom is the *crunkest* place in the universe.

Where else can you speak to mountains by faith and have them be removed? (See Mark 11:23.) Where else can you walk on water? (See Matthew 14:29.) Where else can you find money in a fish's mouth? (See Matthew 17:27.) Where else can you find agape, unconditional love? (See Romans 5:8.) Where else can the dead be resurrected? (See Hebrews 11:35.)

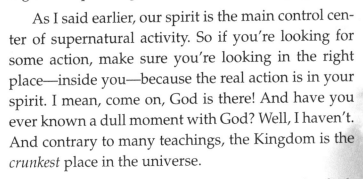

Nowhere! And according to Luke 17:21, this place, this spirit Kingdom, this divine activity, is in you!

Listen, living out of your spirit will not only change your life, it will change the lives of those around you. My husband and I can truly attest to this. As a result of living out of our spirit, we have been able to do movie projects, plays, recordings, books, and many other spectacular things. This has created a platform for actors, singers, authors, rappers, and entrepreneurs to use their God-given gifts and talents for the Lord. Did I mention that we did all of these projects with no bank financing? That's right! Everything we needed was already on the inside of us waiting for us to place a demand on it.

Now in the beginning, of course, we struggled with this truth. We tried to get some investors involved, but God wouldn't allow it to prosper at that time. He wanted us to live from His divine supply. He wanted us to know that anything He calls, He finances. And He did just that.

When we finally drew the line of finality and decided to live from our spirit, God began to prosper what we were doing. We started sowing sacrificial financial seeds, and the rest was history. God opened the heavens over us and smiled on us by releasing ridiculous favor! People, money, location spots, and producers were provided miraculously at every interval. All of this was a result of living out of our spirit, the center of supernatural activity.

Jesus lived out of His Spirit and this is why His ministry was so successful. First, He lived a life submitted to His Father and His Father's mission. Second, He allowed the Holy Spirit to influence every thought, every word, and every action. I mean, every move Jesus made was a Spirit-led move.

In His earthly ministry He turned water into wine, cast out devils, laid hands on the sick and they received healing. He also restored sight to the blind, made the lame to walk again, caused deaf ears to be opened, fed multitudes miraculously, and did many more creative miracles that are recorded in the Bible. (See John 2:1-11; Matthew 9:32-34; Mark 1:29-31; Matthew 9:27-31; John 5:1-8; Mark 6:32-44.)

Listen, this is the pattern we are to follow as born-again believers, a supernatural pattern. And just as Jesus did, we are to live out of our spirits, allowing every part of our being to be led and influenced by the Holy Spirit.

Chapter 6

The Power of What You Believe

I'll never forget the day the Holy Spirit said to me, "Your belief is more powerful than you know." I sat there for a moment, thinking, pondering, and meditating upon this simple yet profound truth. It was so true. It seemed like I experienced a quickening moment where scales were immediately removed and I could see for the first time how powerful my belief system was.

I began to do some backtracking in my life. It was like a movie playing in my mind and I could see that many of my life experiences had been directly linked to how I believed. My financial state, my emotional state, and so many other things were directly connected to how I believed. I could clearly recall events in my life where I believed that things would not go well for me nor work out for my good. And guess what, those things did not work out. It was not because I was a bad person, not because I had done something wrong; I just didn't believe that any good would come my way. I didn't understand the power of my belief.

Whether you are aware of it or not, you have a belief system in place that is running like software every minute of your life. It is an unseen designer, constantly working in conjunction with your thoughts and words, creating your next experience. Based on information you've seen, heard, and experienced, your belief system drafts out life plans that become the blueprint for your reality. Remember this, because something you believe is creating your life experiences.

Now I don't believe that everything that happens in life is a direct result of something believed. For example, let's say someone goes to the doctor for a routine checkup and discovers that he or she has cancer. Now, the average person doesn't go to the doctor anticipating or believing that he or she will be diagnosed with cancer. What has occurred is simply a breakdown somewhere in the body; it is not linked to this individual's belief.

But take a person who has always believed and spoken that he would have cancer simply because his mother, father, or grandparents had it. This individual, if he continues to believe this, think this, and speak this, will most likely at some point in his life experience exactly what he believed was going to happen. This person wouldn't be shocked at all if he was diagnosed with cancer. Now I didn't say he wouldn't be worried or sad; I said he wouldn't be shocked. This is simply because he believed it to be, long before it manifested. His experience was a direct result of what he believed.

Do you see the difference? Let's go to the Word of God and see what it says about the power of our belief.

And Jesus said unto the centurion, Go thy way; and as thou hast believed, so be it done unto thee. And his servant was healed in the selfsame hour (Matthew 8:13).

He that believeth and is baptized shall be saved; but he that believeth not shall be damned. And these signs shall follow them that believe; in My name shall they cast out devils; they shall speak with new tongues (Mark 16:16-17).

But when Jesus heard it, He answered him, saying, Fear not: believe only, and she shall be made whole (Luke 8:50).

For what saith the scripture? Abraham believed God, and it was counted unto him for righteousness (Romans 4:3).

But the scripture hath concluded all under sin, that the promise by faith of Jesus Christ might be given to them that believe (Galatians 3:22).

These Scriptures prove that if you want to experience the power of God, then you must believe that this power not only exists, but it is available to you and for you. This is the only way to unlock this supernatural power flow in your life. See, I believe in the supernatural power of God; therefore I experience supernatural manifestations in my life. I believe in supernatural debt cancellation; therefore I have experienced supernatural debt cancellation on several occasions. I will experience what I believe.

This is why Jesus came on the scene preaching the Kingdom of God. When we believe what Jesus preached and taught, we will experience what Jesus said we would experience. But we must believe first or have faith in the King and the existence of His supernatural Kingdom. For in the Kingdom of God all things are possible.

Are you hearing me? There is a life bigger and far greater than the one you are experiencing! You are one belief system away from seeing the greatest turn-around of your life if you believe and receive what I am saying. You can change your belief system through the power of the Word of God, the Holy Spirit, and the application of some simple natural steps.

Listen, the same way you got that old defeated belief system is the same way you get the new super-natural one. Faith comes by what you hear, according to Romans 10:17. All of our lives we have been hearing and observing things that have directly affected and shaped that which we believe. Parents, peers, schools, churches, radio, movies, music, and television, to name a few, have all played a part in shaping that which we believe about God, ourselves, and about others.

For example, I was raised in an environment where people thought in a limited way, which therefore produced lives that were limited. The phrase "I can't" seemed to be the theme song of not only our home, but also those around us. As I grew older, this Limited Belief System stuck with me, for it had been established and had taken root at a very young age. This Limited Belief System would constantly tell me

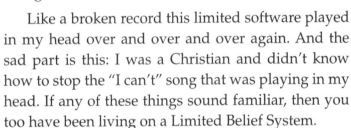

what I couldn't do: "You can't afford this, Lynetta, and you can't afford that. You can't write a book, you can't make an album, you can't get healed, you can't start a business, you can't go on vacation, you can't go shopping, you can't give because you can't afford to, you can't fill up your gas tank, and you can't go to college!"

Like a broken record this limited software played in my head over and over and over again. And the sad part is this: I was a Christian and didn't know how to stop the "I can't" song that was playing in my head. If any of these things sound familiar, then you too have been living on a Limited Belief System.

The good news: this Limited Belief System can be removed and an Abundant Belief System can simply take its place. I like to call it supernatural software. By hearing what the Word of God says about you and voicing what the Word of God says about you on a regular basis, your life can be transformed. Romans 12:2 calls this process renewing the mind. When you renew your mind you are simply reshaping the way you believe and think. Change in life will require a change in both the arena of belief and thought, for they are products of the same reality.

Listen, if my life can change, so can yours. Now this change in my life didn't happen by itself and it didn't happen overnight. It has been a process and has required both my active involvement and the Holy Spirit's help. The Holy Spirit will work in us and with us to bring about transformation if we really want it. However, He will not do it for us. There is a part that we play in the transformation process.

If you are truly ready to change your life, then prepare to change that which you think and believe. Don't forget that something you believe is creating, designing, and drafting out your next life experience. This is why you will want to aggressively engage in your transformational process by investing time in reading the Word of God, hearing of the Word of God, and voicing of the Word of God. *You must hear yourself speak.* First Peter 3:10 (AMP) says:

> *For let him who wants to enjoy life and see good days [good—whether apparent or not] keep his tongue free from evil and his lips from guile (treachery, deceit).*

From this verse we can clearly see that if we plan on enjoying life and seeing good days, we had better say the right things. Our happiness in this life is directly connected to the words that come out of our mouths on a daily basis. This is because our words are a direct reflection of that which we believe. Apostle Paul wrote in Second Corinthians:

We having the same spirit of faith, according as it is written, I believed, and therefore have I spoken; we also believe, and therefore speak (2 Corinthians 4:13).

Quick Tips

1. Decide what you want.
2. Believe that you can have it.
3. Receive it as yours.
4. Voice it in faith.

So don't forget this. Yes, read books, go to conferences, listen to anointed ministers and teachers—but also remember that your tongue is a producer working in conjunction with your belief system helping to bring about your next life experience.

Chapter 7

Word Shift

Life shifts require word shifts. A shift in words is a shift in thought flow. A shift in thought flow is a shift in life—for the current of life moves in the direction of the dominant thought. Therefore by changing what I say, I change what I hear, thus affecting how I think and believe. As a result, life moves in a different direction, causing me to reap different results.

Words are spirit seeds, transcendental products of the supernatural realm. When used for good, they create life-giving events and occurrences. When used for evil, they become death agents orchestrating catastrophic life events and occurrences.

This power has been placed within us as spirit agents. Proverbs 18:21 tells us that this death and life power resides in our tongue or in the words that we speak. Therefore the power to change our life course is strategically connected to our beliefs, our thoughts, and our...*words*.

As a wife, mother, minister, and life coach, the words I speak must be carefully chosen and thought about. Like a skilled wordsmith, I must choose wisely that which I speak and decree in the lives of those I serve and love. This is because words are spirit seeds; therefore they have the power to impact our life success at unimaginable, unseen levels.

These spirit seeds called words are influencers that help to form, paint, and imprint mental images in our minds. Marketing companies understand this concept very well. They understand that if the right images are not erected in the imagination of the audience they are trying to reach, then there will be no success. And no success to them means no financial profit. Therefore they invest millions of dollars in what I call word marketing campaigns. They know that by choosing words that compel and motivate, the right images will be painted on the canvas of the consumer's imagination, thus creating a psychological connection that causes the consumer to desire that which is being sold. This is the genius of successful marketing companies.

We too must become skilled in the way we use our words. Too often people are turned off from the message of the Gospel of Jesus Christ simply because of the way we communicate it. Our words many times are poorly thought out and chosen; therefore they erect nothing in the individual's imagination and interest. Smart Kingdom Marketers know that what we say and how we say it makes the difference.

For my husband and me, the message of Jesus Christ and the supernatural Kingdom is real. Therefore we find it easy to minister to people about Jesus and His Kingdom. And get this, people in the world actually listen to us. The majority of our coaching clients are not Christians. They are business professionals, professional athletes, and entertainers, just to name a few. They know where we stand concerning our faith and yet choose to come anyway. Many have given their lives to the Lord and have experienced a complete life turnaround. This is simply because God sends to us those He wants us to minister to and we share the Gospel in an irresistible manner. Oh, I love that, Holy Spirit…the irresistible Gospel of Jesus Christ.

Today, I want you to take inventory and really look at the words that you speak on a daily basis. I want you to examine the words that you say about yourself and others. Are they death-laced, poorly chosen words that have killed your drive, esteem, hope, happiness, and courage? Or are they words that give hope and build you and others—life-giving words that cause you to awaken every day with vigor, vitality, and power? Please examine this often overlooked area because your words are either drawing success to you or pushing success away from you.

Here is something I did to change the results I was getting financially. My husband and I were struggling in the area of saving and investing money. Well, of course, God showed us that we would have to become better stewards by investing financially into His Kingdom work and investing naturally. But He also showed us how to change our words to reap better results financially. Instead of using the word *budget*, we replaced this word with the word *vision*. In our minds when we heard the word *budget*, we felt restricted and locked in. By replacing the word *budget* with the word *vision*, a different image was erected in our minds, freeing us from limited thinking in the arena of our finances. As a result, we now give some, save some, invest some, and spend some. A shift in words caused a shift in thought flow. And a shift in thought flow resulted in a shift in life.

Chapter 8

Faith Expressions

I am going to open this chapter by simply saying, *your faith must be expressed!* Because faith expressed is belief in action.

James 2:20 tells us that *faith* without *works* is *dead*. This simply means that what you believe cannot stand alone. It must be accompanied by an action or expression. This is what I call "faith expressions." See, when you express something you are communicating or acting out that which you truly believe. This is real faith.

Thousands of Christians do not understand this power principle. They say they are walking by faith but there is no evidence of their faith. God requires faith! Hebrews 11:6 tells us that it is impossible to please Him without it.

Real faith is belief in action or belief expressed. Abraham believed God and expressed it by offering his son Isaac upon the altar (see Heb. 11:17). Noah believed God and expressed it by building an ark (see Heb. 11:7). I could go on and on, but here is my point. Faith without works is dead faith, for it stands alone. Real faith is belief in action or belief that is expressed.

As citizens of a divine Kingdom, our faith must be expressed in the earth realm. People must see the reality of this Kingdom through the faith of its citizens. One of the ways that people can see this is by the love we have for one another. Loving the Lord with all of our hearts and loving one another is the highest expression of our faith. The way we talk is an expression of our faith. The way we live is an expression of our faith. The way we give is an expression of our faith. The way we treat people is an expression of our faith. Everything we do is communicating what we truly believe to the world around us.

This revelation has changed my life, because I now know that I can't please God without faith and that I must add action to my faith. This is what all the financial sowing has been about in my life. I didn't get it at first and honestly thought that the only thing the preachers wanted from me was my money. There was a time I even thought God was trying to take from me. No, He wasn't. He was trying to add to my life by giving me principles by which to live. And one of the principles had to do with learning how to express my faith through giving. This pleases God.

Let me give you an example. My husband and I wanted to sell our car. It was older but still in working condition. So we decided to sell it and use the money to pay off some debt. Well, the first thing we did to express our faith was to give voice to the desire of our hearts. We released "now faith" by speaking that our car would sell within the next 24 hours. By the next day our car still hadn't sold. But we kept on speaking that within 24 hours our car would sell. Finally there was someone who expressed interest in the car, but the deal fell through. Then someone else expressed interest in the car, but due to a lack of money, he wasn't able to purchase the car.

A whole month passed before I realized I had not expressed my faith with a financial seed. Yes, my husband and I had spoken it, believed it, and received it as done, but we forgot to *seal the deal* with a financial seed. Now, I am not saying that to sell your car or your house you have to sow a financial seed. But for me and my husband the sowing of financial seeds has always enabled us to break through barriers and into manifestation.

Well, we knew which seed to sow for it was a seed principle the Lord had revealed to us years prior. It was a secret weapon in our arsenal that we had only shared with a few people. This secret seed weapon had enough potent power that, when sown, things would change many times within 24 hours. Barriers, obstacles, and hindrances would move the moment we sowed it. I will go into greater detail regarding this seed principle later in this book.

So we sowed our seed in full assurance that the deal was now properly sealed. It wasn't but a couple of days later that my husband sold that car. And get this, we received $300 more than what we originally asked.

No, we didn't buy a blessing, for it is impossible to buy the blessings of the Lord. The Word of God says He gives us all things freely to enjoy (see Rom. 8:32). My responsibility is to just express faith in what has already been promised. The sowing of our words, prayers, and finances are simply ways to express our faith in God. It wasn't the sowing of money that moved God; it was our faith in what He told us to do that moved Him. Because remember, it's impossible to please Him without faith (see Heb. 11:6). And by putting an action with what I believe, I am saying to God, "I believe You, I trust You, and I have nothing to worry about."

Chapter 9

Mental Designing

Over the years I've made some pretty amazing discoveries. But one that tops my list is the discovery of a divine creative tool called the mind. Now I know I've mentioned the mind throughout these writings, but in this chapter I will be specifically showing you how to use this tool to create, draft out, and design the life you really want through a process that I call mental designing.

The word *design* means "to create, fashion, execute…to make a drawing, pattern, or sketch of."[1] But this word also means "to conceive and plan out in the mind."[2] And this is exactly what mental designing means. It is simply a creative process in which one intentionally designs, creates, and drafts out on the neutral ground of the mind that which he desires to enter his life.

It has been said, by whom I don't know, that what I want to enter my life must first enter my mind. I agree with this saying simply because every great design was once a citizen in the province of the mind. For that which we see physically was first spirit (image) substance, formed, fashioned, and drafted out in the mental realm.

Images, or what I call spiritual imprints, can quickly take physical form and make a grand entrance into our lives physically. This is why it is vitally important to guard that which enters the gate of the mind. For every image that enters the province of the mind has the potential to become part of your life. In the same way that a camera has been designed to capture images, so can the mind.

I would like you to take a moment and examine your overall image patterns. By this I mean take a good look at what you think about the most. For that which is in abundance in the mind, will be found in abundance in one's life. Remember, life moves in the direction of the dominant thought. This is simply because the mind, being that it is neutral, believes that the images or the spiritual imprints that have been allowed to enter are the directives that you desire to move in.

As citizens of a divine supernatural Kingdom, we must lock into this truth and begin to use this divine creative tool called the mind to add to our lives and bring us into greater levels of manifestation. We must leave systems of default and become aggressive and intentional, directly applying this principle to our lives.

The Mental Designing Process

Now that you have a basic understanding of the creative potential of the mind, let's put it to work for our good. As I stated before, mental designing is simply the creative process in which one intentionally designs, creates, and drafts out on the neutral ground of the mind that which he desires to enter his life.

So step one in this process is to decide on that which you desire to be a permanent part of your life. Be specific and very clear for generalities and vague abstract mental images are enemies to manifestation.

For example, you desire to own a spa salon or film company. Well, don't just say, "I desire to own a spa salon" or "I desire my own film company." Learn the art of specifics by saying, "I have my own spa salon located in Atlanta. My salon looks like a vacation resort with palm trees, water fountains, and life-giving paintings on the wall. I have a health bar located in the salon. Fresh island drinks (non-alcoholic) are served and I offer child care so mothers can relax at my beautiful spa salon. People come from all over the world to patronize me and my salon. It has often been said that one visit changes your entire life. My spa salon is like no other salon in the world. I have healing rooms where people enter and immediately sense the presence of a real God and are healed. I even have heated floors that massage the feet. My staff is well paid, and I am a godly servant leader who treats those who work for me with the utmost respect. I offer them insurance and benefits. People love to work for me. I am a faithful tither and giver to the work of the Lord. Father, I thank You for my wonderful spa salon."

I know this sounds a bit extreme, but I wanted you to capture the image in the mind through the art of being specific. Of course there are other factors involved, such as business plans, location, licensing, etc. But in this chapter I want you to learn how to design in your mind that which you desire in your life first, then take the natural steps that need to be taken to *close the deal*.

Second, do what I call "capture the image." This is the part where daily—or as often as you can remember to do so—you should replay what you want to be part of your life, over and over and over again in the mental realm. By repeating this process, you are creating a rhythm that plays the same every time until image formation has occurred. Habits are results of behavioral rhythms. In other words, habits—whether good or bad—develop by what one does over and over and over again. For example, the image of the spa salon shouldn't be thought about once but should be pondered upon and meditated upon habitually and daily.

Now one warning—don't make the process hard by trying to force or make something happen. If it enters your mind, it has the potential to enter your life, almost effortlessly. For the mind is a divine creative tool. Put the right images in it on a consistent basis, and your physical life becomes a reflection of what you designed in the mind.

Third, hold on to the captured image. You have the blueprint; it is the image that you have captured in your mind. This blueprint is the pattern from which you build. Holding on to that image, gather the things that you see in your captured image. This is the secret behind every great designer and the designs they create. They build by spirit pattern, holding on to what they saw first in the mind.

One last thing I would like to share about the power of mental designing is that you can apply this process and do what I call *kill the giant* and *diminish*

the mountain. The reason I would like to share this is because far too many citizens have allowed debt, bill collectors, and many other things to be magnified larger than what they are in the mental arena. I too am guilty. But I learned that I could use my tongue and my mind to take my power back from the enemy.

Numbers 13:33 says:

And there we saw the giants, the sons of Anak, which come of the giants; and we were in our own sight as grasshoppers, and so we were in their sight.

This verse is a perfect example of how things are magnified in the mental arena, causing us not to pursue our enemy and fulfill all that God has called us to fulfill. These spies were sent to check out the land that God had promised to give them. God Himself in Numbers 13:1-2 told Moses that Canaan had been given to them. But because the wrong God-image and self-image had been erected in their minds, they came back with an evil report that basically said they couldn't take the land even after God had told them that it was theirs. Their words were mere reflections of what they believed and what they had designed in the mental arena.

However, in the camp were two men of a different sort: Joshua and Caleb. They had the right image of both God and self imprinted upon their minds.

Therefore they were able to speak the language of victory.

Victory of any sort is first won in the mind. *If you don't win it in the mind, you rarely will get it in life.* For example, as long as you are designing bill collectors' victory over you, then you will constantly feel powerless to them and do nothing to change your situation. Year after year passes by and nothing has changed. This is not because God doesn't love you; this is simply a case where the wrong images have been imprinted on the mind about yourself and the situation. You have captured an image of defeat, and this image has taken form and has entered your physical world.

But giants can be slain and mountains can be removed. Faith-filled words will be your number one weapon to use in this process. Add to that a divine creative tool called the mind and you've got a formula for success. You can actually kill giants and diminish mountains through the de-magnification process. De-magnification is the process in which you remove your focus entirely from the problem. In this way you are stripping the object of its power. Your mouth no longer discusses it and your mind no longer thinks it. After you de-magnify what you no longer desire to be part of your life, shift your focus from the problem to the answer. Focusing on the answer enlarges its size and its power in the mental arena. Take your focus off something and the object diminishes in both size and power.

So remember that yes, you can mentally design what you desire to be a permanent part of your life. Just don't make the process hard by trying to *force* or *make something happen*. If it enters your mind, it has the potential to enter your life, almost effortlessly. For the mind is a divine creative tool. Put the right images in it on a consistent basis, and your physical life becomes a reflection of what you designed in the mind.

Now let's take our design and write it down.

Endnotes

1. *Merriam-Webster Online Dictionary 2011*, s.v., design, http://www.merriam-webster.com/dictionary/design (accessed January 5, 2011).

2. Ibid.

Chapter 10

Pen Power

Did you know that when you write something down, it is more likely to come to pass than if you don't? Makes you think, doesn't it?

As a spiritual life coach, I am adamant about giving my clients life-altering tools that enable and empower them to reach phenomenal life goals and dreams. Some of the tools that I use in life transformation sessions are paper and an often overlooked item called an ink pen. That's right, simple paper and pen can bring about a change in one's life.

There is genius found in simplicity. Many people never discover it simply because it is not complex enough to satisfy their complicated quest and desire for knowledge and insight. But oh how God uses the simple things of life to hold powerful truths and revelation.

For the past few years I have been using paper and pen as creative life weapons to unlock powerful manifestations and life events. One event in particular was where I used my pen to unlock a supernatural manifestation of money. I mention this in the "Messages in the Night" chapter, but here's a recap. In the dream, I received information that money was being given away to women, and all I had to do to receive it was to write what I needed on a colored piece of paper. Then, in the dream, I wrote everything I needed on the colored piece of paper, and within minutes, the money was in my hand. It was just that simple.

When I woke up the next morning, I ran to the store and followed the instructions of the dream—I believe in acting out what I've seen in the spirit realm (provided, of course, that it is aligned with God's Word and will). I found the same colored paper that was in the dream and wrote down specifically what I needed. That same day my husband and I received $1,000 supernaturally. It was the exact amount that I had written on the paper.

Now, one experience doesn't constitute a pattern. For something to be a pattern, it must be repeated over and over and over again. Scripture is full of

God's patterns. We as citizens must discover these divine patterns and principles and align with them to reap maximum Kingdom results.

After the initial experience, I began to wonder what else I could do with pen and paper. So I decided to try to manifest a desire through the art of writing things down. I started with something as simple as writing down the type of day I wanted to have. I got up early and wrote in my journal all the wonderful things that I wanted to see manifest that day. These, of course, were things within reason. As a result, my day mirrored that which I had written. It was unbelievable! I mean, all this time paper and pen were hidden weapons, tools of creativity to help manifest desires.

Habakkuk 2:2 says, *"And the Lord answered me, and said, Write the vision, and make it plain upon tables, that he may run that readeth it."* This Scripture proves that writing things down plays an intricate part in the manifestation process. For instance, goals when written are more likely to be achieved simply because there is a map to follow. What we write serves as a map providing clarity to where we're going and how we're going to get there.

Writing things down also provides a channel for our thoughts and desires to leave the mental realm and enter the physical, or the realm that we can see with our natural eyes. Many times our thoughts and desires are sort of vague and abstract. The process of bringing them from the mental realm to the physical will help eliminate that which is not clear. There have been many times in my life where clarity came as a result of continuous writing.

Because of the awesome results that I've experienced with writing things down, I would like to share with you something that I do each and every year on the last day of that year. You must do it prior to the entrance of the new year.

I buy a journal to *write forth* my year. No, that's not a typo. We all are familiar with the term *speak forth*. I *speak forth* and *write forth*, meaning I prophesy with pen and paper what the year will manifest in my life. Of course this is done after I've prayed for God to reveal His plans for that year. After praying, I grab my paper and pen and I start releasing what I believe to be God's will for that year. Of course there is God's general will, which we find in the Bible clearly laid out for us. But then there is His customized will that has been designed for me as an individual. I write both His general will and His customized revealed will.

As I *write forth* in faith, I believe that which I've penned has already happened; therefore it has no choice but to manifest itself in my life. By writing it down I am simply legalizing its entrance into the physical realm.

Listen, don't make this some religious duty or thing that you do. Religious people complicate everything, draining themselves of vitality and power. Simply begin the process with an open mind, enjoying the therapeutic life-changing power and rewards of writing things down. If you find yourself upset and moved by contrary life winds, grab your journal and a pen and simply start writing. I use this process as a means to unclutter my mind and create flows of creativity all the time. So don't forget to write, using your *pen power* to manifest what you desire.

Chapter 11

Pray-N-Go

Pray-N-Go sounds more like a gas station than a chapter in a book. And that is exactly why I named this chapter Pray-N-Go. I wanted to take us from the traditional, ritualistic, boring regimen of religious prayer and move us into a lifestyle of power praying with results following.

In concept, Pray-N-Go simply means this:

- Sow the seed of prayer in faith.
- Give thanks to God, knowing that everything that you prayed for was in agreement with His Word and will for your life.

- Receive it as done.

- Then go about your day.

Prayer is a lifestyle for me. It's not a ritualistic, religious, boring thing I do to get stuff from God, although I do reap amazing benefits as a result of praying. As a matter of fact, prayer is such an integral part of my life that many times I'm praying and not even realizing that I'm doing it.

When I coach people, I'm praying. When I'm ministering, I'm praying. And when I'm writing, I'm praying. This is because prayer for me is simply staying in communication with the Father throughout my day with both my words and my thoughts. For example, when I have a client who calls and needs my help, I immediately shoot a thought prayer to Daddy asking for His help and His wisdom in the situation. And guess what? He responds. The Holy Spirit communicates divine intelligence to me and gives me a solution.

It's sad to say, but many of our churches have not taught prayer in an irresistible manner. It has not been taught in a way that appeals to the imagination, causing one to desire it or to engage in it. This is one of the reasons that prayer is one of the least attended meetings in some of our church services. I didn't say *all*; I said *some*.

I remember when I first started teaching on prayer; it was boring and quite religious. The reason is that, as a leader, I personally did not have a real understanding of prayer. Therefore I could only teach it from the level that I understood it. Something amazing happens to ministries when the leader, the set man or woman of God, moves beyond the simple reading of the letter and begins to experience the breath of the Spirit upon the letter. For it is then that the leader can impart what he or she has experienced and that which is now real to them.

Now as a leader when I pray or minister on prayer, amazing things happen. People are healed from diseases, lives come to Christ, marriages are restored, purpose and destiny are revealed, hindrances are removed, and breakthrough occurs. This is because now I'm praying with both understanding and revelation.

Prayer serves as a supernatural bridge that connects us to God, who is Spirit. This divine system of communication has been designed by God Himself as a means for us as His sons and daughters to talk to Him about anything and everything that concerns us. Not only does prayer provide a divine line of communication for us to communicate our desires and needs, but it also allows God to share with us what He wants done in the earth realm. Nothing happens until someone sows the seed of prayer.

I am asked quite often: what is the secret to a powerful prayer life? Well, the Scripture spells it out quite plainly. A powerful prayer life flows out of a relationship with the Father. This is clearly seen in the life of Jesus Christ. Kingdom power flows out of relationship, not religion, not formula, not ritual, but relationship with the Father of miracles. Simply spending time with God will catapult your prayer life to new faith levels and supernatural dimensions. Now let's take a look at the process of prayer.

When the Holy Spirit first revealed the concept of Pray-N-Go to me, He used the principle of seed-time and harvest. Genesis 8:22 says, *"While the earth remaineth, seedtime and harvest, and cold and heat, and summer and winter, and day and night shall not cease."* Prayer is the seed; sow it in faith, asking in Jesus' name, and you will reap a harvest. The only condition is that it must be in agreement with the Word and the will of God for your life individually.

See, prayer runs on a cycle. There is the sowing of the prayer request or petition, which is your seed; your prayer seed enters a chamber called time and undergoes a process; then there is a harvest or the manifestation of that which you prayed for initially.

When your prayer seeds are aligned with both God's Word and His will for your life, something supernatural occurs. Awareness is the key. When you become aware or conscious of that which is going on around you, your confidence increases even more and your faith will be fortified. This is simply because you become aware or conscious of small things, almost insignificant things growing in what I call your life garden. These small things are what the Bible refers to as blades in Mark 4:28: *"For the earth bringeth forth fruit of herself; first the **blade,** then the ear, after that the full corn in the ear."* This Scripture reveals the process of how a seed grows. And part of that process is the breaking forth of the blade first.

When blades break forth in my life after I have sown prayer seeds, I know that I'm in the harvesting cycle. For example, when I pray for loved ones to be saved, I know that this is a prayer that is in direct alignment and agreement with both the Word and will of God. Therefore I can expect results as long as I stay persistent, not swayed by what I see naturally, and continue to give thanks knowing that it's already done.

In one instance, a few days after praying for a loved one who was not saved, I received a call out of the blue from that particular person. At the time he had not given his life to the Lord; he was just calling because he was thinking of me.[1] Coincidence? No, I don't think so. This is a direct result of my prayer seed. The call from this loved one is a blade, or a sign that the harvest is on its way. It may be awhile before the seed produces the full harvest, but I am confident that God heard me when I prayed. Therefore the blade is a sign for me and helps me to continue to stand in faith for what I requested and communicated to the Father.

Every seed, including prayer, has to go through a process. Now there have been times when my husband and I have seen prayer seeds yield a harvest in as little as 24 hours. But please hear me, this will not always be the case. For there have been other times when our prayer seeds didn't yield the full harvest until months and even years later. The key to standing through those times was that we knew that our prayer seeds were prayed in faith and in direct agreement and alignment with God's Word and will for us as a couple. That is what gave us the confidence to continue standing.

There were times when our faith was challenged. Demon agents from the dark kingdom would transmit thoughts of doubt and fear to our minds trying to get us to forfeit what we were standing for in faith. But thank God for the prayer ministry of the Holy Spirit, who, according to Romans 8:26 helps us in our infirmities or weaknesses and makes intercession for us.

Please remember that your prayer seeds must be in agreement with both the Word of God and His will for you individually. For example, when my husband

and I first launched our ministry, everything started out really well. People were being healed, set free, delivered, saved, and baptized in the Holy Spirit. These types of manifestations flowed gracefully and consistently in our ministry. About a year later, we moved into a building, and things began to change. The flow of power that had once accompanied our ministry was gradually dissipating. We experienced some manifestation but not like we had before. So we began praying, asking God to pour out upon the house. I mean, we prayed and prayed. We prayed for laborers to come and help, we prayed for finances, we prayed for restoration, but nothing seemed to be happening.

A short while later, I started receiving night messages, dreams that housed information about the ministry and what was really going on. Then God sent two prophets to confirm that which He was showing me in the spirit realm via the channel of dreams. God revealed to us that we were running the wrong type of ministry. When we started, we were more of an apostolic and prophetic training center. When we transitioned into the building, we tried to run the ministry the way we had seen other churches in our area run theirs. But that wasn't God's plan for us. We had been called and chosen to run a training center model of ministry, not a traditional church. And this is why we weren't prospering.

See, you can pray all day, but are you sowing prayer seeds that align with both the Word of God and His will for you individually and corporately? Dr. Mike Murdock says that the only place your success is guaranteed is in the area of your assignment.[2] My husband and I were not aligned correctly both in purpose and prayer. James 4:2-3 calls this praying amiss. Praying amiss is the result of not knowing how to ask and what to ask for.

When you pray amiss, you are not praying in agreement with both the promises of God and the customized will and plan of God for you as an individual. Therefore you don't reap the benefits. This is why it is vitally important to study the Scriptures so that you will be familiar with the voice of the Holy Spirit and that which has been promised in God's Word.

"And all things, whatsoever ye shall ask in prayer, believing, ye shall receive" (Matthew 21:22). And this is why God couldn't bless what we were doing. It was simply because it was not His will for our lives. We had not been graced at that time nor called to run a traditional church. Our grace was in an entirely different measure of rule. We would prosper traveling the country preaching, teaching, coaching, and running a Kingdom training center where people would learn how to apply Kingdom principles to their lives and get results.

The Bible speaks of many different types of prayers. I cover these powerful prayer types in my workbook entitled, *When a Prophet Prays, Amazing Things Happen*. But in this chapter, I wanted to simply lay a basic foundation regarding prayer. My goal was to paint a picture on the canvas of your imagination that would motivate and strike passion and a desire to pray. My prayer is that this goal was accomplished.

Saints, without prayer seeds being sown in faith, there is no change in the earth realm. Nothing happens in the earth until someone prays. Nothing will happen in your life until you sow the seed of prayer. Nothing will happen in your marriage until you sow the seed of prayer. Nothing will happen in your local church or ministry until the situation is dealt with in the spirit through prayer. Nothing, and I mean absolutely nothing, will happen until we, God's people, pray.

Endnotes

1. To protect the privacy of the loved one I am referring to in this example, I have refrained from using his or her name. In addition, my use of the masculine pronoun is arbitrary and does not necessarily indicate that the person I am referring to is a man.

2. Mike Murdock, *101 Wisdom Keys,* (Wisdom International, 1994).

Chapter 12

Ride the Wave of Grace

Hebrews 4:16 says, *"Let us therefore come boldly unto the throne of grace, that we may obtain mercy, and find grace to help in time of need."* For years this Scripture was just something I read. My heart and mind made no mental connection with its meaning, and therefore I deemed it as just another wonderful Scripture in the Bible. But in the plan of God a time of revealing had been scheduled for me—a time where I would be introduced by the Holy Spirit to the true essence, meaning, and power of Hebrews 4:16.

I'll never forget waking up early one morning with a strong desire and a rather unusual urge to write a book. At this point in my life I had never written a book. Yes, I had penned songs and poems but never a book. Well, that was all about to change.

I walked over to my computer and just looked at it for a moment. Something was stirring inside my belly. It felt almost like running water. I knew within myself that something was about to erupt. I felt as if something was demanding to be brought forth from inside me, almost like a pregnant woman feels her baby pressing to be born. Having given birth to three children, I knew what that felt like. When the water breaks, the baby is coming and there is nothing you can do about it.

I positioned myself to type, almost unaware of what I was doing. It seemed like something was divinely leading me. I opened a new computer file and knew exactly what to call it: "The Perfect Law of Liberty." I looked in amazement, finally realizing that a supernatural transaction was taking place. It was so amazing! All of a sudden the words began to pour out of my spirit. I was typing faster than I ever had before. I could feel the anointing in me and upon me for this book.

I spent the next few hours in this place—a place that I now call God's grace dimensions. No phones were ringing, the kids were still asleep, and the environment was infused with a peace beyond my natural understanding and comprehension.

A short time later, I felt this supernatural power lift. As it lifted, I felt almost sad because I didn't want it to leave. I wanted this presence to literally penetrate every part of my being and every part of my life. But as the earth reality kicked in with the sounds of the phone ringing and the children jumping on their beds, laughing, screaming, and playing, I knew that I had to get back to Earth and prepare breakfast for the kids. But as I prepared to get up, I realized something: I had completely finished an entire book! *The Perfect Law of Liberty.* "No way," you might say! Oh yes, I had written a book, riding the supernatural wave of grace.

Although the book is only 30 pages in length, I have received several testimonies from people who have read the book and received supernatural healing in their bodies and deliverance in many areas of their life. What was interesting though was how they reported reading the book. All of the ones who received these supernatural manifestations reported that they read the book out loud. Yeah, that's right, OUT LOUD!

One lady from Africa brought the doctor's report to one of our meetings and read the results. She said she read the book out loud and received healing from breast cancer. Many other testimonies have been reported and recorded. We now tell people who purchase the book to read it out loud and believe God for the miraculous to take place.

That day the Holy Spirit wanted me to not only see a manifestation; He wanted me to experience a manifestation that would affect me at such a level that I wouldn't be able to forget it. That day, through His power, I stepped into a dimension called grace. This dimension is where God's supernatural ability goes to work on your behalf. It's where things are made possible through His dynamic activity and His divine enabling power.

Walking in the Spirit and riding the wave of grace are synonymous. They both denote God-dependence. When I am walking in the Spirit or living by the Spirit, I am living a life that is totally dependent upon God. There is no dependence upon my own power, talents, or skill, for my trust is in the Lord. This doesn't mean that I am not aware that I have talents, gifts, or enablement; it simply means that I don't depend upon them for supernatural success. My help comes from the Lord who is the giver of the talents, gifts, and enablement.

The Holy Spirit and grace work together, enabling us to live out the plans of God. They empower us to reap dynamic Kingdom manifestations and phenomenal life results.

This truth is proven in the Book of Zechariah which says:

*Then he answered and spake unto me, saying, This
is the word of the Lord unto Zerubbabel, saying,
Not by might, nor by power, but by My spirit, saith
the Lord of hosts. Who art thou, O great mountain? before Zerubbabel thou shalt become a plain:
and he shall bring forth the headstone thereof with
shoutings, crying, Grace, grace unto it* (Zechariah
4:6-7).

Here, the Lord was saying to Zerubbabel that not
only would he accomplish the task at hand of rebuild-
ing the temple, he would do it by Spirit power. Zerubbabel would ride the wave of grace and fulfill what
God told him to do.

See, riding the wave of grace is simply receiving
this power as a gift, in spite of our own shortcomings
or imperfections. Because it's a gift, we don't have to
work up something to get it through human power
or effort. All that is required is that we receive the gift
and be willing to obey the instructions. Romans 11:6
(NKJV) says:

*And if by grace, then it is no longer of works; oth-
erwise grace is no longer grace. But if it is of works,
it is no longer grace; otherwise work is no longer
work.*

As Kingdom citizens, our responsibility is to
receive and permit to operate both the gift of the Holy

Spirit and the gift of grace. The Greek word for grace is *charis,* meaning "gift or favor." And supernatural living will require these two power gifts to be in full operation at all times along with our faith, for they are supernatural forces, spirit agents from the divine Kingdom of God that help us to fulfill both the Kingdom mandate and agenda.

This is proven in Hebrews 2:9, which says:

> *But we see Jesus, who was made a little lower than the angels for the suffering of death, crowned with glory and honour; that He by the grace of God should taste death for every man.*

Jesus' arrival on Earth didn't just happen. It was a strategic, well-mapped-out, divine Kingdom plan designed to save humankind and restore us back to our rightful place in the Kingdom of God. This agenda or Kingdom mandate was accomplished and fulfilled as a result of Jesus' obedience to His Father, His submission to the Holy Spirit, faith, and the full operation of grace. For the Bible says that He tasted death for everyone by the *grace* of God.

Riding the wave of grace is one of the most rewarding Kingdom benefits. This power gift enables you, along with the Holy Spirit who is also referred to as the Spirit of grace, to fulfill and accomplish amazing supernatural things. A revelation of grace will catapult your life to new faith dimensions. You will find yourself accomplishing that which seemed impossible simply because you received the gift of grace and allowed it to fully operate in your life.

One last example of the gift of grace in operation in my life was when I was invited to be on TBN. The host wanted me to be her guest and talk about being a female preacher and a filmmaker. She also requested that I bring a movie trailer so she could promote the film.

After hanging up the phone, I called my producer and asked him to make me a shorter trailer that could be used on the show. We already had a trailer, but it was three minutes in length. I needed a trailer that was about a minute long. My producer agreed and told me that we could pick it up later that evening.

Later that evening my husband picked up the shortened trailer, and I watched it. Unfortunately, it wasn't at all what I had in mind. According to our arrangement with TBN, we were supposed to drop off the trailer first thing the next day so it could be reviewed and prepared for the show, but now I didn't know what I should do. I wasn't an editor and sure didn't know anything about putting a movie trailer together. On top of that, I didn't even have editing equipment.

I sat there for a moment. Discouragement tried to creep in when all of sudden I had a God thought: Boldly come to the throne of grace to receive mercy in my time of need. Now, I've done some pretty amazing things in the past through the supernatural power of the Holy Ghost. But this would top them all!

I asked the Holy Spirit to help me, and guess what He did. Although I had no formal editing experience, the Holy Spirit graced me and showed me how to edit the clips and put together a movie trailer on a simple laptop! Did you hear me? Through the grace of God, I was able to ride the wave of grace and complete a task that I had no knowledge or formal training in!

I'm pleased to report that the TBN interview went very well. The viewers loved the trailer, and as a result, our ministry received numerous calls about both our training center and the film. This was clearly a connected work of both the Holy Spirit and the gift of grace. I chose to lean on, have faith in, and totally depend upon the Holy Spirit; and as a result, grace, favor, power, and supernatural ability to accomplish what I couldn't accomplish in my own strength or in my own power was released to me. This grace release had nothing to do with merit or what I deserved. It was simply God's nature at work, manifesting itself in the form of grace.

Chapter 13

Supernatural Momentum

"Today, I choose to rise above my fears, step out on the dream God placed in my spirit, and ride the current of supernatural momentum."

Webster's dictionary defines *momentum* as a strength or force gained by motion or through the development of events. It is both power and energy that is released to those who move out and move toward a desired end. Movement is the seed that triggers the release of supernatural momentum.

To have a dream is one thing, but to move toward the fulfillment of that dream is an entirely different ball game. For there are two types of people in the game of life: there are talkers and there are walkers.

Talkers discuss events. Walkers create the events that "talkers" talk about.

God has placed a dream inside you. This dream is in seed form and will require both knowledge and understanding of the role that supernatural momentum plays in the fulfillment of that dream. Yes, there are other factors involved in the dream fulfillment process, but we will be specifically discussing the principle of momentum.

As stated earlier, momentum is defined as a strength or force gained by motion or through the development of events. Many people never experience the release of supernatural momentum simply because they do not get started. They want momentum before they begin; but momentum is built over time and intensifies through the development of events. Momentum grows, increases, and enlarges in the lives of individuals who have chosen to engage in the dream process even if all the pieces are not in place.

Details can be an enemy to your momentum. Yes, I believe in counting the cost, and I believe in having a detailed plan. But if all you focus on are details, then there will be no room for divine creativity to flow. And if there is no creative flow, there will be no momentum. We must learn to bridge details, creative flow, and momentum. And like a symphony, there should be a synergetic flow among all three.

I said earlier that movement is the seed that triggers the release of supernatural momentum. Many of our lives, churches, and businesses appear to be lifeless entities because of a lack of supernatural momentum. For years I didn't see any progress in my personal life, my ministry, or my business. I had great ideas but I was too afraid to move out on what God had placed in my spirit to do. And as a result the dream seed stayed in the realm of the spirit waiting to be released.

It took me awhile, but through the power of the Holy Ghost and the Word of God I was able to break through fear. And let me tell you, when I broke through, I really broke through! Since 2005 I have authored three books, ghostwritten books for other authors, recorded a second album, launched a marketplace training center, and wrote and produced two full-length movies. Somebody say, Hallelujah!

Please don't think that I am boasting in my own accomplishments. I am well aware that I would have never completed any of these tasks without the Word of God, the Holy Spirit, grace, faith, my husband, my kids, my family, my team, and supernatural momentum. As I tenaciously stepped out on what I believed to be the dream of God, I experienced the force, energy, power, enablement, and motivation that supernatural momentum releases. I found myself flowing in a supernatural current of momentum.

I am convinced that these things would have never occurred if I hadn't made a choice to step out on what God placed in my spirit each and every time. I didn't allow my creativity to be clogged by getting stuck in the details. I knew what it was going to take and chose to engage anyway by faith. As a result the fruit can clearly be seen not only by me, but by others.

Listen, movement is the seed that releases supernatural momentum. And if you're going to experience any type of success in this life, you must choose to engage in the process by simply getting started. For example, if your desire is to write a book, then do some research on book writing. After that, open a word file on your computer and just start typing. If you don't have a computer, then buy a notebook and a pen and start writing your book. Do you know how many times I sat at the computer not having any idea what I was going to write? But I would just start typing anyway.

Most of my manuscripts make no sense in the beginning. I have topics everywhere, chapters are all out of order, and I'm not clear yet on how everything is going to gel together. I just know that I have a desire to write a book. As I continue in the process of fulfilling this desire to write a book, things begin to gel together and make sense. The Holy Spirit begins to divinely infuse my mind and spirit with ideas, divine insight, and information. Sometimes this process takes a few days and other times it takes a little bit longer. But as I stay in that creative flow, supernatural momentum starts erupting in me and around me. The help I need, the pieces I need, all begin to fall in place.

So let's remember today that movement is the seed that releases supernatural momentum. If you want to experience strength, power, divine flow, and enablement, then you must choose to step out on the dream God placed in your spirit. Don't wallow in details. Pay attention to them, but do not allow the details to take your creativity hostage and stop the flow of the divine in your life.

Chapter 14

But What if I Fail?

"Today I make a decision to do something. Even if I fail, at least I did something...."

Failure is when something does not accomplish its intended purpose. While there are other ways to define *failure*, this definition clearly indicates that what happens in our lives, or the events that take place, do not define who we really are as individuals. This is significant because many times—because of our limited beliefs about ourselves—we attach failure stigmas to our lives and allow others to do the same.

I believed for many years that I was a complete failure. This belief was based upon what I had heard growing up, the mistakes I had made before I gave my life to Christ, and the mistakes I made after giving my life to Him. I felt I couldn't win for losing. When things didn't go as planned, I would always find a way to associate the failing of the event with who I was as an individual, thus placing a failure stigma on my life.

This went on for a while, but I thank God for His delivering power. As I cried out to the Lord for help, the Holy Spirit stepped in and began to minister to me in a profound way about who I was as a spirit being, His role in my life, and my new position in Christ Jesus. The more He would communicate to me who I was and what Christ had done for me, the more freedom I began to experience. My confidence began to rise and the stigma of failure was gradually dissipating and a new identity, a whole new belief system, was emerging.

My training didn't stop there. The Holy Spirit began giving me simple tasks and assignments to fulfill. I didn't know it at the time, but these tasks and assignments were being used as tools to empower me from the inside out. Yes, they were teaching me how to follow the Holy Spirit, but they were also sharpening my spiritual and natural skills, building my confidence, reshaping my core beliefs, and establishing a firm foundation in the Gospel. This process, which was done over and over and over again, was establishing a strong spiritual root system of faith that the enemy would not be able to penetrate. And when the storms of life would blow, I would still be standing because of the foundation and the roots that had been laid in my life.

As a result of this processing, failure is no longer part of my current reality. Reality is defined as that which is real to you. In my world, failure does not exist; it is a nonexistent force that I no longer entertain nor give a place. This is simply because my core beliefs have changed. Now I only believe that all things are possible in Christ Jesus (see Matt. 19:26), and that it's impossible for me to fail.

When demon spirits transmit failure messages to my mind, such as "something is going to happen and things are not going to work out," I don't receive them. Why? Because they are lies and there is no truth in these messages. My mind then goes to work for me and not against me, working in conjunction with my new core beliefs, which are "all things are possible in Christ Jesus and it's impossible for me to fail." As a result of believing and thinking this way, I now live a life that's void of failure and full of the God kind of success.

Proverbs 23:7 says that *"as* [a man] *thinketh... so is he."* This simply means that we are products of our thoughts. Therefore we become what we think about the most. This is why Joshua 1:8 instructs us to keep the Word of God in both our mouth and in our thoughts; pondering, meditating, giving thought to and obeying that which is being read. For this is the only path to true success.

The reason I said *true success* is because there is real God success that comes as a result of speaking, meditating upon, and adhering simply to the Word of God, or the instructions of God. In contrast, there is also the *illusion* of success. This type of success only looks like the real deal—meaning people can appear successful simply because of the car they drive or the house they live in. But if that house and that car have been gained by means that are outside of the laws of God, then it is not good success; it is the illusion of success. Listen, failure is an option. An option is a choice. If you fail in this life as a Christian, it is because you choose to fail. So, don't choose to fail. The Holy Spirit is not a spirit of failure but a Spirit of victory, wisdom, power, and success. He will teach you how to profit and have the God kind of success. And guess what? The person of the Holy Spirit is in you.

So don't be afraid of taking some risks. Many times we don't take risks because we know that we become exposed to loss. But I'd rather become exposed to loss than spend my entire Christian life too afraid to go after the dreams God has placed in my heart.

My husband and I have lost many material things over the years simply because we decided to pursue our dreams. We placed more value on what we believed God wanted us to do than on the earthly possessions that we had. Many people laughed at us. And there were those who wanted to see us fail. But because we chose to believe, "All things are possible in Christ Jesus and it's impossible for us to fail," we are walking in a powerful breakthrough anointing today. As ministers and life coaches, we are helping many others find the courage to rise out of fear and failure and go after what God has placed in their hearts to do.

Of course we're not saying that everyone reading this book should quit his or her job or leave the church to pursue a dream. What we are encouraging you to do is to no longer allow the thought of failure to have rule over you. Work your job until God says it's time to come off. And make sure it's God when you hear it. Remember that your job is a tool, and if you have no seed to sow, you have no harvest to receive. Also let's remember that our jobs provide us with wonderful evangelism opportunities.

Second, please do not leave your local church because you have a dream in your heart for ministry. Wait, be patient, and be properly released by God and the anointed leadership He has placed in your life.

I heard someone put it like this: "Life is God's gift to you, but what you do with it is your gift back to

Him." Listen, you will have some challenges in this life, for the Word of God says that you will. But the Word of God also offers encouragement by saying that Jesus Christ has overcome the world (see John 16:33). So don't be afraid to step out, take some risks, and make some bold Spirit-led moves. Don't worry about failing. If you have consulted with God and with anointed wise counsel, then go for it!

I personally believe that you have failed only when you don't try. So, I don't care if things end up a flat-out mess or you make a thousand mistakes. Get up, wipe the tears from your eyes, and learn from these mistakes. For mistakes are stepping stones—if you learn from them, they will help promote you.

Remember that failure is an event, it is not who you are. So whatever you do, don't stop pursuing what God has placed in your heart.

Chapter 15

Magnet to Opportunity

Preparation is a powerful life force. It's like a magnet, drawing into its orbit opportunities and doors. When people prepare, they position themselves first, then allow the reality of what they are expecting to catch up later.

As you read this book, I realize that you have dreams, desires, and aspirations. But dreams don't just happen. They are products of the spirit realm; therefore your natural alignment and participation is going to be vital to the manifestation process. And this is where preparation comes in. Let me give you an example.

After I had my second son, I desired a daughter. So, the day my son was born, I spoke out of my mouth, "Three years from now, I will have a daughter. She will have dimples like her daddy and curly hair." From that day forth I would say, "I am having a daughter. She will have dimples like her daddy and curly hair." Three years later, I went to the doctor one afternoon and found out I was pregnant. Of course the doctor didn't know yet if it was a boy or a girl. But I told my doctor that I knew. I shared with my doctor that I would be having a little girl with dimples and curly hair.

After leaving the doctor's office I did two things. I called my husband and told him I was pregnant, and I headed to the department stores and started shopping for my little girl. I did this continuously and consistently. There was not one time that I even considered buying boy clothes. Why? Because I was not preparing for a little boy. I was preparing for my little girl with dimples and curly hair.

Well, my daughter was born later that year in the same month that my son was born. Remember, I sowed the word seed three years prior. This is why my daughter, with a dimple and curly hair, was born in the same month as my son. His birthday is October 5 and my daughter's birthday is October 19. Was this a coincidence or was this the natural working of a higher spiritual law?

A few years later, I wanted to move into a bigger house. We had outgrown our quaint little condominium and desperately needed something bigger and better. I knew that I could have the house I wanted according to the Word of God, and I knew just how to get it.

First, we found the house we wanted, got some boxes, and started declaring and preparing. We cleared out old stuff and made room for new things. We declared and prepared every day for eight months before we saw a physical manifestation. It was a lengthy process, but the timing was perfect.

When we moved into the house, one of the first things that God did was increase us financially by giving my husband a nice raise on his job. Second, our car note was miraculously cancelled. God was literally freeing up our money in every possible way.

The reason I mentioned the financial increase was because our house note was $600 more than what we had been accustomed to paying in the condominium. The move into the house was a move of faith that helped us to expand not only our minds but our pocketbooks.

Listen, there are things you will never experience if you don't choose to prepare yourself first. You do this by directly aligning with what you desire. For example, if you desire to move out of the projects and move into a nice home, don't just sit there waiting for your ship to sail in. Create the ship by preparing for what you want. Start with prayer and the Word of God. Ask the Holy Spirit to guide you. From there, get up and start looking for the house you want. Go into areas that you know you can't afford. This process expands your mind. Notice I didn't say buy a house you can't afford; I said go into these areas and just allow your heart to be filled with something bigger and better than where you are currently. Don't worry, the Holy Spirit is going to lead you.

Next, get some boxes and start packing. This is an act of faith that says, "I'm expecting to move into my beautiful house this year that God is going to provide." Declare and prepare every day. Begin working on your finances and credit. Go to the furniture store and pick out the furniture that you desire. Continue tithing and giving offerings. Just stay in the flow, because spiritually something is happening; it's just that you don't see it yet. Don't worry about seeing it at this point; just know that the law works. Just keep preparing and declaring and allow the natural working of spiritual law to magnetize to you that which you have prepared for.

Your participation through preparation will be key to your manifestation. Because remember, preparation is like a magnet, drawing to you opportunities and doors. This means that in order to see your desires manifested, you will need to position yourself *first*. This is the process where you dress the part long before you have the role. This is where you believe it to be, long before it shows up in your life naturally. This is where you go first with absolute confidence, knowing that reality will catch up later.

Chapter 16

The Realm of Choice and Judgment

Over the years I have made some good decisions and over the years I've made some pretty bad ones. There were times when my judgment was sound, clear, and directly aligned with the Word of God. But there were other times when my judgment was distorted and somewhat twisted.

One day I was casually reading the Word of God. I wasn't looking for anything in particular; I was just feeding my spirit the supernatural Word of God, when I came across a simple yet profound Scripture in the Book of John. I kept reading this Scripture over and over and over again. I must have spent an entire day pondering on this one truth.

Finally something clicked. I knew that the Holy Spirit had shined light upon His Word so that I could see the truth and incorporate it into my life. The Holy Spirit searches the heart, and my heart had been crying out for a long time for answers and supernatural solutions for life's problems. And one of those problems lay in the realm of choice and judgment.

John 5:30 was the Scripture that the Holy Spirit used that day. Let's read it in three different translations so that we can gain and grasp a firm understanding of how Jesus processed information and made choices. Let us read:

I can of Mine own self do nothing: as I hear, I judge: and My judgment is just; because I seek not Mine own will, but the will of the Father which hath sent Me (John 5:30).

I can't do a solitary thing on My own: I listen, then I decide. You can trust My decision because I'm not out to get My own way but only to carry out orders. If I were simply speaking on My own account, it would be an empty, self-serving witness. But an independent witness confirms Me, the most reliable Witness of all (John 5:30 MSG).

I am able to do nothing from Myself [independently, of My own accord—but only as I am taught by God and as I get His orders]. Even as I hear, I judge [I decide as I am bidden to decide. As the voice comes to Me, so I give a decision], and My judgment is right (just, righteous), because I do not seek or consult My own will [I have no desire to do what is pleasing to Myself, My own aim, My own purpose] but only the will and pleasure of the Father Who sent Me (John 5:30 AMP).

From this Scripture passage, we can clearly see that Jesus was only interested in one thing, and that was fulfilling the will of His Father who sent Him. He boldly declares and acknowledges right from the beginning of the verse that He can do nothing independent of His Father.

As citizens of a divine Kingdom, we too must incorporate this truth into our belief system. If we are going to experience supernatural power and manifestation on a daily basis, we will have to consciously decide and boldly declare that we can do nothing independent of God. A declaration of independence from God will place you directly in a demonic realm of choice and judgment. You will see things from a flawed, distorted, twisted, and unscriptural perspective that will directly affect your judgment.

Judgment is a tool that helps us make choices. It is defined as the cognitive process of reaching a decision or drawing conclusions. If our judgment is just and sound, we will be able to assess situations in life and draw conclusions that are scripturally based, perfectly sound, and reap a wonderful harvest of good in our lives. If our judgment is not just, we will find ourselves reaping a harvest of unwanted and undesirable life results.

Judgment and hearing work intricately together. If you hear the wrong thing, your judgment—or the process by which you reach a decision or draw a conclusion—will be off, thus causing you to continue in the vicious cycle of making bad choices. But if you consistently hear the Word of God, your judgment will be *just*, rightly aligned with the Word and the will of the Father, and you will find yourself making good choices instead of bad ones.

I recall a bad business decision I made that resulted in my husband and me losing $40,000. Everything about the deal looked good and sounded good. So, I prayed about it and asked the Lord to show me what to do. Well, He didn't waste any time responding to me. Every time the guy would come around, I would hear the words *liar, liar* in my spirit. This was the Holy Spirit trying to communicate to me that the guy was a liar. But I ignored it simply because I thought it was me being paranoid. I even thought it was the devil trying to steal my blessing through the transmission of demonic messages.

Well, because of the Father's love for me, He sent me another message in my sleep, trying to stop me from doing business with this man. Once again I thought the dream meant to proceed with the deal and everything would work out. Well, everything didn't work out, and my husband and I lost $40,000 in a deal gone bad. This loss set us back for months, and it was the mercy and grace of God that kept us and restored what we lost.

But here is my point. Because I sought my own will and not the will of the Father, my judgment was off. Yes, I prayed about the deal, but I didn't adhere to what the Spirit of the Lord was saying. I explained earlier that judgment is a tool that helps us make life choices. It is the cognitive process of reaching a decision or drawing conclusions. I came to the conclusion to proceed with the deal because of the information I had heard and processed. My bad choice was a direct result of bad judgment. If I had been a little more patient and sought the Lord a little longer, I'm sure that I would have come to a different conclusion. My choice would not have stemmed from bad judgment but good and just judgment that was directly aligned with the perfect will of the Father and not my own.

Remember what Jesus said in the Gospel of John:

> *I can of Mine own self do nothing: as I hear, I judge: and My judgment is just; because I seek not Mine own will, but the will of the Father which hath sent Me* (John 5:30).

Let us follow this example, this pattern for supernatural living, by first deciding and declaring to do absolutely nothing independent of God the Father. Second, let us forsake our own will, our own way, and our own agenda and fully embrace the perfect will, the perfect way, and the perfect agenda of the Father, remembering that sound and just judgment is a result of seeking the will of the Father and not your own. This is a powerful supernatural key.

Chapter 17

The Prepared Place

"Today I make a conscious decision to be a steward of the goods of God. For I am a Prepared Place!"

I'll never forget hearing these words one Sunday morning in a training class: "Give everyone in the room $25…. You are a Prepared Place." Without hesitancy I consulted with my husband and we obeyed what we believed to be the voice of the Holy Spirit. We felt led to wait until everyone had sown their financial seeds. After this we began to pass out $25 to every student in the room.

As we passed out $25 to all the students, we saw expressions of shock, amazement, and tremendous gratitude upon their faces. We heard some say, "I had just given my last and look what God has done."

Others said, "I wanted to go to the movies; thank You, God." Others cried, simply because the Lord had provided for them that day.

Now of course we know that $25 is not a lot of money. But the Holy Spirit wanted my husband and me to see a powerful truth. When we arrived that morning, we had no idea that the Holy Spirit would lead us to sow $25 into the lives of all the students. Neither did the students know that they would be receiving $25. They were simply coming to class to hear the Word of God. But here is the revelation: Provision from God has already been prepared; God just needs a channel.

The word *prepared* means to make ready, fit, or suitable beforehand. It also means to be fully equipped, ready to handle a task or tasks assigned or entrusted to us. So when the Holy Spirit told me that I was a Prepared Place, He was simply saying that I was a vessel or a channel that was fully equipped and ready to handle the task that God would present to me. The task presented to me that Sunday morning was to sow $25 to all the students. Why? Because in God's eyes, I was a Prepared Place, a vessel that was fully equipped and ready to handle the task that He would present to me.

I didn't feel like a Prepared Place, and my situation sure didn't look like I was a Prepared Place. And frankly, if I had looked at this situation from a natural standpoint, I would not have had the courage or the faith to obey the instructions of the Holy Spirit that day. But because I chose to look at things from the spiritual standpoint of faith, I was able to be a blessing to many people that day.

We must remember that God declares the end from the beginning. In Judges 6:12, the angel of the Lord called Gideon a mighty man of valor. But Gideon was poor and the least in his family. On top of that, he was a coward. So why did the angel of the Lord still call him a mighty man of valor? The angel called him this because Gideon really was a mighty man of valor; he just didn't know it at the time. Therefore God spoke to his potential and caused a line to be drawn between that which Gideon was experiencing naturally and that which God had called him to be.

When God called me a *Prepared Place* that Sunday morning, He was speaking to my potential or speaking to what He had purposed, intended, and equipped me to do. This intended purpose was written before the foundations of the world, and the process that I was going through was simply the evolving of events that would help me discover what was already written about me.

See, I had always had an innate desire to help believers come out of oppression, especially in the financial arena. I just didn't know that this desire had been strategically placed inside me by God. It was part of my calling. Therefore the continual events that would evolve in my life had to deal with learning to live supernaturally especially in the area of finances.

So that Sunday morning when the Holy Spirit told us to sow $25 to the students, it was actually God commanding us to function out of an anointing of more than enough. He knew what He had placed inside me and my husband. But He wanted us to know. He wanted us to live out of our spirit and clearly see that when He tells us to do something, we have nothing to worry about. He wanted the students to see that every need has already been supplied. You may not know what channel He will use, but provision has already been prepared.

This revelation of being a *Prepared Place* has changed my life. And it has caused me to become a radical giver of the *goods of God*. Psalm 24:1 says, *"The earth is the Lord's, and the fulness thereof; the world, and they that dwell therein."* Therefore all that I have is the Lord's. Body, soul, spirit, money, cars, homes, it doesn't matter; it all belongs to the Lord. My responsibility is to steward the goods, affairs, possessions, and business of our Lord until His return. This means I give at the command of God because He's the owner. And there are great Kingdom benefits awarded to those who choose to embrace this concept and live out of it.

My husband and I constantly walk in supernatural favor, supernatural access, and supernatural breakthrough. And we know why: we are one of God's *Prepared Places*. I mean everywhere we go we experience favor, access, and breakthrough. We have experienced some tough times, but God has always provided us with favor, access, and breakthrough.

We have seen God's provision come through some pretty strange channels. But who cares about the channel? The Lord is the Provider. And when God is Jehovah Jireh (your Provider), it's impossible to run out because He's the God of more than enough. Yes, we may get challenged, but we won't run out! As long as I am one of God's *Prepared Places*, functioning as a steward of His goods, He is going to be adding to me constantly and continuously.

Addition in the Kingdom is always a by-product of aligning directly with God's principles or *God's way of doing things*. And subtraction in the Kingdom is usually a by-product of *our way of doing things*. Subtraction is the process by which something is taken away, reduced, or made less than. Of course there are times when God will use the process of subtraction to remove people, places, or things that mean us no good. But usually if one is experiencing subtraction in their lives and not addition, it is simply because there is a preoccupation with "getting" and no adherence to the law of "giving." People who live this way do not understand how God works. Therefore they spend their Christian lives worrying, fussing, and toiling over *things*. My husband and I did this for many years. And in my opinion, to worry over *things* is one of the most debasing things a blood-bought believer can do. Why? Because God told us and showed us how to get the things we desire and need.

Listen, use your gift of choice and make a conscious decision to do things God's way and allow Him to add to your life. Matthew 6:33 in The Message Bible says (I'm paraphrasing a bit) that *we should steep ourselves in God-reality, God-initiative, and God-provisions, not worrying about missing out. For as we do this, we will find that our everyday human concerns will be met and provided.*

God's promises are true and God will not lie to us. His laws were designed to help us and not hurt us. So today, choose His law, His way of doing things, by becoming a steward of the goods of God. Allow Him to take your life and make something awesome out of it. Allow Him to use you to empower others. Allow Him to use you as a *Prepared Place*, a vessel that is fully equipped and ready to handle the task that God presents and a channel through which blessings flow.

Chapter 18

Deliver Me From Oppression

"Today God has delivered me and my household from affliction and He has opened my ears to His instructions."

Oppression is a controlling demon spirit that tries to keep you down by force. It weighs heavily on both the senses and the spirit, robbing you of vitality and life. When this spirit is working, you begin to feel pressed under, weighted, heavy, not able to rise, lifeless, bent over, and stuck! But no matter how intimidating this force may appear, it is no match for the divine Word of God.

Job 36:15 says, *"He delivereth the poor in his affliction, and openeth their ears in oppression."* The first part of this Scripture clearly states that God will deliver those who are suffering and in distress due to the adversity they are facing. The second part of Job 36:15 tells us that God will give the poor instructions, solutions, principles, keys, and answers that move them out from under the demonic power of oppression and places them directly in a divine flow of miracle manifestations.

Demon spirits respond only to the Word of God. This is proven both in Scripture (see Matt. 8:16) and in the example I used in Chapter 4. I was dealing with a financial oppressive spirit. I felt hopeless and weighed down. At this point the Holy Spirit kicked in as a result of my crying out to the Father and gave me what I call a God thought. In other words, He did what Job 36:15 promised He would do. What was that? He promised to deliver the poor from affliction and open their ears in oppression. He opened my ears in oppression by giving me a God thought, or an instruction that would change my situation. I heard it, I saw it, and I moved on it.

Now, I want you to remember something. Whenever you have a God experience like this, it is vital that you pay attention to what happened. Many times we fail to mentally connect with what happened and we forget how we received the victory. This is important because there will be *a next time*. This means the enemy will try you again, most likely in the same area. But, if you paid attention in the last battle, you will most likely know what to do in the next one. Of course there will be times when God will change the instructions, but for the most part, continue in the truth that was revealed.

Our house note was due, and we didn't have enough money to pay it. Now don't forget that I am in training. The Holy Spirit has been dealing with me for months now in the financial arena. And to be properly trained I would have to face adverse situations over and over and over again until I got it. Adverse situations in the Kingdom of God, I now know, are opportunities to apply my faith and receive a God manifestation.

So, as I said earlier, we didn't have enough. I stood in the kitchen cooking when all of a sudden I heard the Holy Spirit tell me to sow a specific amount. Don't forget Job 36:15 says, *"He delivereth the poor in his affliction, and openeth their ears in oppression."* I recognized the voice as that of the Holy Spirit for I had heard this same voice speak to me many times before. Therefore I proceeded to share with my husband what the Holy Spirit had instructed me to do. My husband agreed, and the rest was history.

Later that evening one of the members of our ministry called and told us that she and her husband wanted to be a blessing to us and wanted to sow a $1,000 seed into our lives. My husband and I looked at each other in awe and began to praise God for that which He had done. We were almost dumbfounded at how quickly this seed turned things around.

A few weeks later another financial need arose. At first we worried, but then faith kicked in, and I found myself wondering if I could sow the same type of seed that the Holy Spirit had instructed me before and reap similar results. Something in me knew that I could, but my mind at the time was working against me. This was simply because I had not renewed my mind in the financial arena. Therefore my mind would work against me and not for me in this area. But that was all about to change.

In spite of all the doubt and the mental reasoning that was going on in my head, I pressed forward and sowed the seed—the same type of seed that the Holy Spirit had instructed me a few weeks prior. And, you better believe it, a harvest came in, and it came in quickly.

I mean, I couldn't believe it. In all my years as a Christian I had never experienced so many consistent results in my finances. Things were working so well that I began to say things like, "As quickly as I let it go, overflow." I mean this thing was absolutely amazing. And get this. I was actually enjoying sowing this *strange seed.*

The reason I call it strange is because I had never heard of this type of seed before. Yes, I heard the preachers tell us to sow finances, but I always found myself confused about the acceptable amounts. So my husband and I would just give our tithes and sow anything in our offerings. There wasn't any passion and there sure wasn't any faith. But not with this type of seed. This baby had life-altering power in it. I mean, one day things could be going bad, then all of a sudden, sow this seed and things would change. Things would just start moving in a favorable direction. And let me say this again, we were actually enjoying it.

A short time later we found ourselves back in need and want again. Our faith was challenged in the financial arena, so we decided to break the power flow and stop giving the "strange seed." And once again we became needs-driven not Spirit-led. As a result, that same old spirit came back.

Now please remember, we were still tithing. That was one thing that we did continue. But for us, God wanted our revelation to go beyond religious tithing. He wanted us to enter a realm of abundance through the giving of not only the tithe but of this powerful "strange seed" that He had specifically revealed to us for our individual unique situation.

Well, we did finally get it. We finally realized that what the Holy Spirit was attempting to reveal to us was God's customized plan and design for our lives individually. He wanted us to not only see this truth, He wanted this truth incorporated into our lives as a lifestyle, not just something we practiced here and there. And because we didn't lock in to this truth initially, both in concept and practice, we kept returning to the place where we were being controlled by needs and wants. When we did it God's way, we found ourselves mastering finances instead of finances mastering us.

In addition to understanding our customized design, God wanted us to also understand that money when sown was an act of worship. Money in our lives had controlled us. It held great value in our hearts. So to give it away was an expression of faith and trust in God. In the Bible, the giving of offerings was always synonymous with worship.

He also revealed to us that the force of oppression that had come against us was generational but could be annihilated by using the Word of God and money as weapons in financial warfare.

Now please hear me! What I am talking about in this chapter and in the chapters to follow is our specific, unique, customized design. In other words, this is the way that God has called my husband and me to live. This will not be the case for everyone. This is simply because part of our calling is to bring revelation and deliverance to people who are stuck and in need of direction, especially those who have struggled with poverty. This is one of the reasons our training has been so intense. We have had to learn the ins and outs of how this thing works. Even now we don't know everything, but what has been revealed to us, God has called for us to share in this season and at this specific time.

Please understand that spiritual battles must be fought with spiritual weapons. Second Corinthians 10:4 says, *"For the weapons of our warfare are not carnal, but mighty through God to the pulling down of strongholds."* In this chapter, Paul is defending his apostleship. In doing so, he makes it very clear that we are in warfare and there are weapons involved. These weapons are not carnal but mighty, spiritual, God-designed, and God-infused weapons of spiritual warfare. You may not have realized that you are in a battle. And in a battle you will need the right armor on and the right weapons in hand. Ephesians 6:10-18 (MSG) reads:

> *And that about wraps it up. God is strong, and He wants you strong. So take everything the Master has set out for you, well-made weapons of the best materials. And put them to use so you will be able to stand up to everything the Devil throws your way. This is no afternoon athletic contest that we'll*

walk away from and forget about in a couple of hours. This is for keeps, a life-or-death fight to the finish against the Devil and all his angels.

Be prepared. You're up against far more than you can handle on your own. Take all the help you can get, every weapon God has issued, so that when it's all over but the shouting you'll still be on your feet. Truth, righteousness, peace, faith, and salvation are more than words. Learn how to apply them. You'll need them throughout your life. God's Word is an indispensable weapon. In the same way, prayer is essential in this ongoing warfare. Pray hard and long. Pray for your brothers and sisters. Keep your eyes open. Keep each other's spirits up so that no one falls behind or drops out.

In First Samuel 17:39 we find that David could not wear Saul's armor. A man must walk in an understanding of his own unique, custom-designed anointing. And once again this is what the Holy Spirit was teaching us. Every time we tried to do it another way, we would reap horrific results. Things would *go south* each and every time we chose to wear the wrong armor and fight with the wrong weapons. This was simply because God's custom design for our lives required that we lived supernaturally, using money as a weapon to connect to us God's unlimited supply of abundance.

Now that I have laid a general foundation, I would like to go into greater detail in the next few chapters about money and its purpose according to Scripture. I will also share in these chapters principles that my husband and I have both received and proven in both our lives and in the lives of others. These principles, when applied and incorporated as a lifestyle, will have long-lasting, life-altering power. You will also find powerful, proven testimonies about how these teachings have changed thousands of lives. Are you ready?

Chapter 19

Money Masters

Someone said, "Giving is the only proof that you've mastered greed. Master greed and you can master money."

Merriam-Webster's online dictionary defines greed as "a selfish and excessive desire for more of something (as money) than is needed."[1] When this force is in operation, people quickly find themselves willing to do almost anything—lie, steal, cheat, and work like slaves, it doesn't matter. Because, like an addict, they have been hooked and are now strung out, willing to do whatever is necessary to satisfy the never-ending desires of a bottomless force called greed.

Greed and mammon are products of the same reality. Jesus says in the Book of Matthew that:

*No man can serve two masters: for either he will
hate the one, and love the other; or else he will hold
to the one, and despise the other. Ye cannot serve
God and mammon* (Matthew 6:24).

Webster's dictionary defines *mammon* as the false
god of riches and avarice. Mammon is also a word
used for money or materialism. Although these defi-
nitions are correct, the word itself denotes and is
reflective of the overall force or spirit surrounding
money, wealth, and power, therefore not money itself.
We will go into greater detail a little bit later in this
chapter.

Any deviation from truth is error. This is why we
must carefully pull out the true essence of that which
Jesus was really saying to us in Matthew 6:24. Was He
saying that we couldn't have money or things? Was
He saying that we had to be poor in order to inherit
His Kingdom? Or that being poor was proof of our
spirituality? What was He really saying to us? We will
come back to this passage of Scripture in a moment.
But first, go with me to Luke 18:18-30:

*And a certain ruler asked Him, saying, Good Mas-
ter, what shall I do to inherit eternal life? And Jesus
said unto him, Why callest thou Me good? None is
good, save one, that is, God. Thou knowest the commandments, Do not commit adultery, Do not kill,*

Do not steal, Do not bear false witness, Honour thy father and thy mother. And he said, All these have I kept from my youth up. Now when Jesus heard these things, He said unto him, Yet lackest thou one thing: sell all that thou hast, and distribute unto the poor, and thou shalt have treasure in heaven: and come, follow Me. And when he heard this, he was very sorrowful: for he was very rich. And when Jesus saw that he was very sorrowful, He said, How hardly shall they that have riches enter into the kingdom of God! For it is easier for a camel to go through a needle's eye, than for a rich man to enter into the kingdom of God. And they that heard it said, Who then can be saved? And He said, The things which are impossible with men are possible with God. Then Peter said, Lo, we have left all, and followed Thee. And He said unto them, Verily I say unto you, There is no man that hath left house, or parents, or brethren, or wife, or children, for the kingdom of God's sake, who shall not receive manifold more in this present time, and in the world to come life everlasting.

From the text we can clearly see that this man was very rich. But although he was very rich, he realized that he needed something in addition to the earthly possessions that he had. This is why he came to Jesus.

He wanted to know how to inherit eternal life or the God kind of life.

In response to the man's question, Jesus starts the conversation by taking all attention off Himself and directing it straight to His Father. He then acknowledges that the man knows the commandments, or the basics. The rich man is clearly proud of the fact that he has obeyed the commandments and kept them since he was a youth. I'm sure at that moment he believed that he was about to receive just what he had asked for initially: instructions on how to inherit eternal life.

When Jesus gives the young man the instructions, there is a clear mood shift in the text, for I felt it myself. I believe this man was very sincere. I believe he really wanted to know how to inherit eternal life or the God kind of life. The problem came in when the instructions that Jesus gave required him to give up what was most important, or what held greatest value in his heart, in exchange for eternal life. (Don't forget, this man was *very* rich! And there is a difference between being rich and being very rich.) As a result, the Bible says, the man was very sorrowful because he was very rich. Yes, he *wanted* eternal life, but he wasn't *willing* to pay the price.

The story continues, and if you skip down to verse 28, you will find another man whose attitude and actions were totally different from the rich man's.

This man was Peter, a disciple of Jesus. Peter saw and heard this whole thing go down and obviously realized that there were benefits available to those who had left all and followed Jesus. He realized that he qualified for the inheritance of eternal life simply because he had left all and followed after Jesus Christ, unlike the rich man.

So Peter opened his mouth and boldly said to Jesus, *"Lo, we have left all, and followed Thee"* (Luke 18:28). He was basically saying, "Jesus, what's in it for us?" Now before you get super-religious on me, let's take a look at Jesus' response to Peter's statement in verses 29 and 30:

> *And He said unto them, Verily I say unto you, There is no man that hath left house, or parents, or brethren, or wife, or children, for the kingdom of God's sake, who shall not receive manifold more in this present time, and in the world to come life everlasting.*

In other words, if you put the Kingdom of God first, all these *things* will be added unto you, not just in the life to come, but starting right now in this present time! That is something to shout about!

See, I said earlier that Jesus is not trying to take something from us, He's actually trying to get something to us. He wants us to have money and things in this life, He just doesn't want money and things to have us as they did in the life of the rich man, which was the reason he couldn't sell his goods and distribute to the poor. *Giving* is the only proof that one has mastered greed.

Jesus doesn't want us living as peasants and slaves bound by the pursuit of money and things. Do it His way, which is the Kingdom's way, and money and things will chase us down and overtake us. We end up with both—blessings now and blessings in the life to come.

Beware of Covetousness

Luke 12:15 tells us to *"Take heed, and beware of covetousness: for a man's life consisteth not in the abundance of the **things** which he possesseth."* Covetousness can be defined as a strong desire for what another has. It can also be defined as an envious eagerness to possess something. This force works within the heart and mind of men and women, creating a preoccupation with getting and gaining.

Covetous people trust more in things such as financial institutions, credit cards, investments, wealth, etc. Because they are earthly minded and mammon bound, they place their trust in systems and structures that have the potential to fail. Their happiness, their peace, their joy, their security, and their self-worth are all wrapped up in the *things* they own and possess in the material realm. The danger in this is that material things are temporal. They are not made up of spiritual or eternal substance so they don't last forever; they only last for a moment. This is why Colossians 3:1-2 tells us:

> *If ye then be risen with Christ, seek those things which are above, where Christ sitteth on the right hand of God. Set your affection on things above, not on things on the earth.*

In other words, set or establish and firmly fix your mind, your thoughts, your heart, your desires, and your deep cravings on eternal, godly things, things of substance that will never fail nor end.

Matthew 6:19-24 reads:

> *Lay not up for yourselves treasures upon earth, where moth and rust doth corrupt, and where thieves break through and steal: but lay up for yourselves treasures in heaven, where neither moth nor rust doth corrupt, and where thieves do not break through nor steal: for where your treasure is, there will your heart be also. The light of the body is the eye: if therefore thine eye be single, thy whole body shall be full of light. But if thine eye be evil, thy whole body shall be full of darkness. If therefore*

> *the light that is in thee be darkness, how great is that darkness! No man can serve two masters: for either he will hate the one, and love the other; or else he will hold to the one, and despise the other. Ye cannot **serve** God and mammon.*

Here in Matthew 6, Jesus is not telling us that we cannot have money or things. He is simply telling us not to allow mammon, or materialism, to have us. This is why He said in verse 24 that we cannot serve two masters. The word serve means to devote one's life or efforts to something. It would be impossible to serve or devote one's life to something without some sort of mental grip and emotional attachment. This is simply because of the value associated with that which is being served.

Therefore we are admonished to make a choice, changing our life outlook to one that is eternally driven. For one cannot *serve* both God and mammon. He is showing us a better way that will have powerful, lasting, eternal effects on our lives now in this life and in the one to come.

I mean, look at our society. It has become an empty soul, void of standard and therefore void of power. Driven by a materialistic system and outlook, people are now willing to do anything for money. Many have become servants and slaves to what some call *the almighty dollar*. This love for money and things is the number one cause of divorce and havoc in many of our families. This love for money and things has even crept into the Church, wreaking havoc in every possible way all in the name of Jesus Christ.

To serve money or to serve things is one of the most debasing things we can do as Kingdom citizens. Money is simply a tool or a medium of exchange that can be used to connect us to spiritual blessings and God's abundant supply. Do right with it and you'll reap a good harvest. Do wrong with it and you'll reap a bad harvest. It's just that simple.

We need money in this world to advance the Gospel, take care of our families, and to enjoy other life luxuries. Solomon tells us in Ecclesiastes 10:19 that *"money answereth all things."* Ecclesiastes 7:12 calls money *"a defence."* So money is not the problem. We need money in the world that we live in, and the Bible confirms this. A wrong relationship with money is the culprit. Many love it more than God. This is clearly seen in our society.

As I said earlier, people, including some in the Church, will do anything for a dollar. For example, many citizens of the Kingdom will go out all week and eat; they will labor all week at a job for a paycheck; they'll buy expensive name-brand clothes and shoes; they'll work diligently to get a degree to make more money; but when it comes to God and His global agenda, there is no place in their heart for Him.

When their pastor asks for the church to give a sacrificial offering, they complain. When the church service is two hours long, they complain. When the offering tray is passed around, they grudgingly give $10. These people have their hearts, faith, and trust in the wrong system. For only fools trusteth in money and uncertain riches, but a wise man trusteth in the Lord (see Luke 12:16-21).

Saint of God, if we are going to walk in God's unlimited realm of financial possibilities, our priorities must shift. Our hearts must turn toward the God of true riches and allow Him to bless and prosper us His way. So what if you can't buy a Dolce Cabana purse this week; take that money and invest it in the Kingdom of God. So what if you can't go to Paris; take that money and invest it in the Kingdom of God. Wait on buying that new car and sow that money into the advancement of God's global cause. Kingdom law promises that when we sow faith seeds like this with a correct attitude, then God Himself will make sure that we have more than enough to meet every need—and this includes trips, vacations, houses, cars, finances, etc.

I'm going to say it again: God wants us to have money and things. He just doesn't want money and things to have rule over us. This is why He has designed a powerful, more effective way for us to enter the realm of unlimited financial supply.

Endnote

1. *Merriam-Webster Online Dictionary 2011,* s.v. "greed," http://www.merriam-webster.com/dictionary/greed (accessed January 5, 2011).

Chapter 20

Treasures in Heaven

Recently one of my protégés came to me with a financial problem. She shared with me that she and her husband were really going through a tough time financially and didn't know what to do. They were faithful tithers and givers into the work of God, but something was clogging the flow. As I sat there listening, I could clearly sense that she had moved away from doing something she really loved to do, which was visiting the hospitals and taking care packages to the families of those who were sick. So I asked her a rather unexpected question. I didn't ask her how much money she could sow, for she was already a faithful financial sower. What I asked her shocked her! I asked her, "When was the last time you visited the hospital and took baskets to the families of the sick?" Well, a smile came across her face, and at that moment, she knew which seed she needed to sow: love, time, and care baskets.

A few days later, this young lady called me and shared an awesome testimony about how God turned things around for her financially simply by laying up treasures in Heaven. By seizing the opportunity to visit the hospital and deliver care baskets, she positioned herself to receive God's abundant flow. This is simply because God loves people. Help them, and God will manifest phenomenal things in your life.

Anytime you help people—the poor, the sick, the needy, the single mother, the fatherless, the motherless, the widows, those less fortunate, the prisoners, the bearers of good news—you automatically position yourself to receive God's abundance. Her business turned around not because she was perfect but because she followed a spiritual law.

Matthew 6:19-21 says:

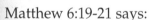

Lay not up for yourselves treasures upon earth, where moth and rust doth corrupt, and where thieves break through and steal: but lay up for yourselves treasures in heaven, where neither moth nor rust doth corrupt, and where thieves do not break

through nor steal: for where your treasure is, there will your heart be also.

We must lay up treasures in Heaven, seizing every opportunity to add to our heavenly store or account. This means: do things on Earth that have meaning and lasting results. For in the life to come you will have to give an account for that which you did while on Earth. For example, when you feed the poor or visit and pray for the sick, you are laying up treasures in Heaven. When you minister salvation to the lost, you are laying up treasures in Heaven. When you give money, time, and talent into advancing the vision that God gave your pastor or apostolic overseer, you are laying up treasures in Heaven.

I tell people that one of the quickest ways to see financial breakthrough is to help the poor and bless your pastors and spiritual leaders. Make sure that they don't have a need of anything. If they are book writers, help them publish their books, then buy several copies when they come out. This helps them continue to advance the message of the Kingdom of God and Jesus Christ. Send them on vacations yearly! If they have some debt, get involved with sowing into their lives to relieve some of the pressures of life. In this way you are laying up treasures in Heaven.

Listen, the reverse of Matthew 6:21 is true also: where your heart is, there will your treasure be also.

Time, money, and resources will always be sown in the area of life that has more value to you. And the area that has the most value to you is the area that has your heart. If your heart is wrapped up in the things of this world, then you will find it hard to invest in things that have heavenly or spiritual significance.

But if your heart is in Heaven, wrapped up in the supernatural Kingdom of God, you will find it easy to invest in its expansion globally. You will use your time, money, and resources as tools to advance the love, power, and message of Jesus Christ. Neither God nor your pastor will have to make or force you to do it because your heart is in Heaven, the place of your greatest value.

Chapter 21

The Strange Seed

As citizens of a spiritual Kingdom we must understand that the laws or the principles by which we live are spiritual. They are not natural laws but higher spiritual laws. When one directly aligns, connects to, and flows with these divine laws, powerful manifestation occurs. This is simply because these laws are designed with us in mind. God strategically set up the system to bless and prosper His people.

For a moment I would like you to use your imagination just like you did when you were a child. Close your eyes and envision having unlimited financial resources to advance the Kingdom of God in the earth. Now imagine having unlimited finances to buy not only homes for you and your family but for other people. Imagine yourself being debt-free and you and your family taking vacations every year. Imagine giving your pastor a check that is so large that it would pay off the church building, pay off his house, pay off his car, and pay off his debt. See your bank account running over with more than enough finances. If you did this little exercise, then you have just entered the realm of unlimited financial possibilities.

It has been said, *if we can imagine it, it can happen. And if it enters my mind, it can enter my life.* In the realm of unlimited financial possibilities, all things are possible. Luke 1:37 says, *"For with God nothing shall be impossible."* This means that with God there is no limit as to what can happen in my life if I believe and deem it possible. Supernatural debt cancellation can happen; I can become wealthy and help expand the message of Jesus Christ globally; I can be a financial blessing to the poor, the homeless, the widows, and the fatherless; I can get that promotion; I can take my family on a wonderful vacation every year; I can buy that house, *IF* I believe that these things are possible. Don't forget, if you want to experience the impossible, then you must believe in the God of the impossible.

What we say and what we do are by-products of that which we believe. This means that if I *believe* in the supernatural power of God, then my words and actions will directly reflect that which I believe. For example, I *believe* that God's system of seedtime and harvest is real. Therefore I give or sow what I desire to be part of my life. I am very conscious of the seeds I sow in thought, word, and deed. Financially, I honor and worship the Lord with my tithes, possessions, and firstfruit offerings because I *believe* that in doing so I will reap the benefits of Proverbs 3:9-10:

> *Honour the Lord with thy substance, and with the firstfruits of all thine increase: So shall thy barns be filled with plenty, and thy presses shall burst out with new wine.*

Now there was a time when I lived under the dictates of a poverty consciousness and a limited system of belief. I viewed life through limited lenses, therefore everything I measured out in thought, word, deed, and faith was limited. Thus, I reaped limited life results. Luke 6:38 says:

> *Give, and it* [that which you give or sow in life] *shall be given unto you; good measure, pressed down, and shaken together, and running over, shall men give into your bosom. For with the same measure that ye mete withal it shall be measured to you again.*

Living in the realm of unlimited financial supply will require that we forsake a poverty consciousness and embrace an abundant way of believing, thinking, and speaking. This will be the only way to sustain the flow of abundance in our lives. In the testimony I gave in Chapter 4 did you notice that when we embraced God's way of doing things, which is the abundant system, and we started giving, we experienced a breakthrough financially, not once, but each and every time we gave? But when we stopped giving we returned to a state of neediness and limited financial provision and flow. We returned to poverty consciousness simply because we had not established an abundant system of believing, thinking, and speaking that could sustain a continual flow of God's abundance.

In God's prosperity plan, we must learn how to give and receive—both are required to complete the cycle of abundance.

God has used *giving* as a means to break poverty consciousness in my life, increase my faith level, and place me in a constant divine flow of abundance and good. For when one's consciousness is filled with abundance, he or she can experience God's unlimited life and financial possibilities. People with an abundant consciousness feel a sense of empowerment when they give, for they know that they won't run out because God and His provision are not limited but unlimited. Individuals who live with a poverty consciousness find it hard to give; therefore they hoard or hold on to that which they have. In doing so they legalize poverty and lack in their life and are not able to reap the Kingdom benefits associated with giving.

> *There is that scattereth, and yet increaseth; and there is that withholdeth more than is meet, but it tendeth to poverty. The liberal soul shall be made fat: and he that watereth shall be watered also himself* (Proverbs 11:24-25).

> *Give freely and become more wealthy; be stingy and lose everything. The generous will prosper; those who refresh others will themselves be refreshed* (Proverbs 11:24-25 NLT).

A revelation of love compels the heart to give. John 3:16 says, *"For God so **loved** the world, that He **gave** His only begotten Son, that whosoever believeth in Him should not perish, but have everlasting life."* Here we see the compelling force of love at work. Love preceded the action to give. Not only did God give; He gave His very best. For without love we have nothing. Therefore love must be the supreme motivator and driving force behind all that we do in the Kingdom.

For many years I gave my time, service, and tithes without love being the supreme motivator or driving force behind that which I did. I had a preoccupation with getting and not giving, therefore I stayed poor. Now that I understand that love must be the supreme motivator and driving force behind all that I do in the Kingdom, I see awesome manifestations. And because of my love for the Lord, my love for people, and my desire to see my Father's Kingdom expanded in the earth, God blesses me ridiculously. I don't chase money; I simply sow it as a seed, and as a result, money finds me. This is simply the natural working of Kingdom law.

Giving has become a lifestyle for me. And as a result, I no longer live my life in default mode, always waiting for God to do everything. I actively engage in that which I want to receive of Him by living what I call a firstfruit lifestyle. A firstfruit lifestyle is just that. It's a lifestyle where I go first in faith, then God responds to my faith.

It took me a long time to get this but I finally got it. Throughout these past 13 years I noticed that not much happened in my life without faith and the expression of my faith, first. Take, for example, the first Gospel album I recorded. I set the date with the studio in spite of the funds not being available. As soon as I scheduled studio time, the finances showed up. This theme has been consistent in my life for the past 13 years. Even financially, in order for us to see manifestation, we have to go first in faith, then we reap the harvest.

For example, do you remember the strange seed I talked about in Chapter 8, "Faith Expressions"? You know, the one that put us in a divine flow of provision every single time? Well, that seed is what I now call the 10 percent principle. God showed me how to sow 10 percent of what I wanted to reap. This was outside of my tithes. For example, if I had a debt that was $500, all I had to do to pay it off was to sow 10 percent of the debt in faith. Once again this would be outside of tithing. The key to the manifestation would be that the 10 percent seed would have to be sown in absolute faith, nothing wavering, and sowed first, beforehand, and in advance for the harvest we desired to reap.

This was different from traditional tithing where we would give God His tenth *after* we received our check. This principle required that we sowed *before* we received the check. Of course there are other dynamics around this seed principle that the Holy Spirit has revealed to me, so before engaging in this type of giving, I recommend that you invest in my book entitled, *Money Is Easy to Manifest.* Now I know that we all are required to sow time, resources, and possessions to help advance the Kingdom of God. But with me and my husband there seems to be a weightier call or gifting in this area, thus making this way of living and giving a lifestyle and not a religious duty or a one-time event.

Now of course we do set aside sacrificial firstfruit offerings for the Lord yearly as practiced in the Bible (see Exod. 23:14-19; Lev. 23:10; Deut. 26). Proverbs 3:9-10 says:

Honour the Lord with thy substance, and with the firstfruits of all thine increase: So shall thy barns be filled with plenty, and thy presses shall burst out with new wine.

For us, honoring and worshiping God this way has always affected our success levels both financially and in our lives personally. Firstfruit living and giving changes not only your finances; it changes your entire life. Doors of opportunity open; joy and peace flow; your marriage is blessed; your children become blessed and doors of opportunity open for them; revelation increases in your life; you receive heightened sensitivity to the things of the spirit; your spiritual ears and eyes open and you begin to hear God more clearly; and you receive an increase in confidence and faith to accomplish your assignment. These are some of the manifestations that we have seen and experienced as a result of living a firstfruit lifestyle.

We could go into greater detail regarding firstfruit giving. But my goal in this chapter was not to go into a long religious dissertation about firstfruits as a religious practice or duty. My goal was to simply share with you that which God has done and is doing in my life, personally. And saints, it's not some religious yearly activity that I participate in to get something from God, although there are benefits. For me, first-fruit living and giving has been about faith and obedience to God. It has catapulted my husband and me out of a default way of living and into a more engaging one that produces far greater life results.

Chapter 22

Money Meets Authority

Now that we clearly understand what money's purpose is, we must become strategic in our giving. This means that we must become wise stewards and wise investors, knowing how, when, and where to invest the money and resources God has entrusted into our hands.

The Bible is clear as to where we are to sow the money that He has entrusted into our hands. He tells us to help the poor, the needy, the fatherless, the widows, and our brothers and sisters in Christ. But these are not the only places God instructs us to put that which He has entrusted into our hands.

Another place that God instructs us to invest our time, resources, and money is in the soil of anointed ministries. I call this *grace targeting*. Grace targeting is a method by which we target an anointing upon a ministry or minister's life by sowing finances or something that is valuable directly into the soil of that ministry. As we sow into this anointing, we sow with an expectancy to receive or partake in the same anointing or the grace that is upon their lives.

God places different anointings or different supernatural grace endowments upon individuals for ministry service. Ephesians 4:11-12 says:

And He gave some, apostles; and some, prophets; and some, evangelists; and some, pastors and teachers; for the perfecting of the saints, for the work of the ministry, for the edifying of the body of Christ.

These are not the only gifts mentioned in the Bible. According to First Corinthians 12, we all have spiritual gifts. Spiritual gifts can be defined as divine energies or operations that enable us to serve or perform ministry service. These gifts work by love and enable us to accomplish extraordinary things in the earth through the strength and power of God. (Visit our Web site to find out more about your own unique spiritual gifts.)

Joanna, the wife of Chuza, Herod's business manager; Susanna; and many others who were contributing their own resources to support Jesus and His disciples (Luke 8:3 NLT).

Although we all have these gifts, not all of us are called to hold governmental Kingdom offices such as apostle, prophet, evangelist, pastor, and teacher. These gifts that were given by Jesus Himself come with some hefty responsibilities, therefore will require some pretty hefty support if they are to accomplish and fulfill that which God has called them to. And this is what we will be discussing throughout this chapter.

Many do not realize the powerful benefits that flow through these gift connections. When connected, these gifts or grace endowments can bring about supernatural results and manifestations in the lives of those who honor them and sow into them consistently and continuously. This is why I always ask people to tell me who God has assigned to their lives to bring them into all that God has for them.

It is amazing to me how many blood-bought believers do not know the answer to this question. As a result, they continue to struggle day to day, month to month, and year to year, simply because they are not aligned with a ministry gift that carries an anointing or supernatural grace for their lives and their situations. Jesus of course is our Bishop, Chief Shepherd, and Chief Apostle. But Jesus Christ Himself gave the Ephesians 4:12 gifts as a means to connect people to His anointing that is housed in these men and women of God.

Throughout the Word of God a clear pattern is laid out for us to follow. The pattern is this: use your resources, things such as time, possessions, and money, as tools to connect you to an anointing or a burden-removing, yoke-destroying power. These things are valuable to us; therefore they can be used as instruments, or mediums of exchange. Take your time, possessions, and money and sow them in faith into an anointing that's expanding the Kingdom of God and you will reap explosive benefits. This is simply because this is how God has designed it.

In First Kings 17 a widow woman experienced firsthand the power of this type of divine connection. When the prophet Elijah arrived there in Zarephath, the widow woman was gathering sticks and preparing to die. But that quickly changed as the prophet gave her an instruction to give him some water and make him a cake *first*.

Notice that his instruction was for her to give him a little cake *first*. The prophet was teaching her a powerful principle of placing God first and obeying His instructions even in the tough times. Take a seed and sow it first to God as an expression of your faith. Then physically sow it or connect it to an anointed ministry gift.

In this case, the widow woman sowed into the life and ministry of Elijah, who was a sent one. He was a prophet of God graced with a miracle anointing. Matthew 10:41-42 (AMP) reads:

> *He who receives and welcomes and accepts a prophet because he is a prophet shall receive a prophet's reward, and he who receives and welcomes and accepts a righteous man because he is a righteous man shall receive a righteous man's reward. And whoever gives to one of these little ones [in rank or influence] even a cup of cold water because he is My disciple, surely I declare to you, he shall not lose his reward.*

This widow woman's life was changed the moment she received the prophet and connected to the anointing through giving. First Kings 17:15 says that the entire house ate for many days, the barrel of meal wasted not, and neither did the cruse of oil fail. This is the prophet's reward. As a result of her obedience and her connection, she experienced not a one-time miracle manifestation but a continuous flow of the anointing and miraculous provision in her life.

God promises those who support His ministers rewards and benefits. In the Book of Philippians we find the apostle Paul's response to a gift that the church had sent him while he was in prison. The church at Philippi knew that the apostle was in prison, so they sent a financial gift by Epaphroditus. In Philippians 4:15, apostle Paul states clearly that no church had communicated with him concerning giving and receiving except them, the church at Philippi. He even goes on to say that they, the church at Philippi, did this more than once. In verse 17, apostle Paul explains that this type of giving wasn't really about him, but more about fruit that would abound to their account. And as a result, apostle Paul declares a blessing over them in verse 19 by saying that God would supply not some of their needs but all of their needs.

Yes, contrary to many teachings, there are benefits attached to assisting God's men and women of God who are advancing the Father's global Kingdom agenda. One of those benefits is that fruit abounds to your account. Another benefit is that you will be able to partake or eat from the anointing or grace that is flowing in their lives. Countless Scriptures prove this truth. This is why you must become strategic sowers, targeting the anointing or the supernatural grace endowments upon men and women of God that He has *sent* and *set* in Kingdom positions of authority. This is simply because when money meets apostolic or *sent* authority, something explosive happens. Let me give you some personal examples.

A couple came to my husband and me with a need. Their credit was messed up and they really needed a vehicle. They didn't want a car because their family was too big. So we began to minister to them about supernatural giving and living. We explained to them that God would meet their need and that there was a vehicle with their name written all over it. We shared with them our testimony and how God had begun to meet our needs above and beyond through giving sacrificial offerings that were above the tithes. We continued to explain to them how the process worked. We explained how the money that they had should be used as a seed and adjoined, connected, and targeted to an anointing or grace that had the power to bring deliverance and breakthrough.

We never told the couple to sow into our ministry. We felt that God should open their eyes and lead them to the anointing that they needed to sow into. Well, within minutes they pulled out a faith offering of $40 and sowed it into our lives. The reason I called it a faith offering was because it was all they had. They shared with us that since we had come into their lives, amazing doors had begun to open. And they wanted to keep that flow in their lives through targeting a financial seed into the anointing of breakthrough, favor, and access that was resting upon our lives.

A few days later, we received a call from the couple. They shared with us how God blessed them with not only an SUV but also a painting contract. We praised God with them but we knew that it was the natural working of Kingdom spiritual law. Take your money and possessions, connect it to an anointing or a supernatural grace, and receive supernatural results.

Another example was when a young lady wanted a home but had recently filed bankruptcy. Through no fault of her own, she had to file bankruptcy and was quite saddened that one of her family members used her credit without her knowledge. She came to us and we prayed for her. We believed that God would do what seemed impossible, for we had experienced so many supernatural manifestations that it was hard for us to believe anything else. We knew that God would give her a house.

Later on, God gave her a faith instruction to sow an extra $100 into our ministry every week for the next couple of months. This would be outside of her tithes. This is the realm of giving you want to get to. In addition to tithing, begin sowing special sacrificial offerings in faith into an anointing or supernatural grace.

I didn't say to remove the tithe; I said in addition to the tithe.

Well, she obeyed and the rest is history. One evening a friend of ours who was a real estate agent visited our ministry. I felt a leading to talk to her about the young lady's situation. She agreed to see what she could do to help. At first it didn't look like she'd be able to do anything, but that all changed very quickly. This is because the young lady didn't know it at the time, but she had consecrated her dream of home-ownership by obeying the voice of the Lord in her giving. Not only did God tell her what to sow; He told her where to sow it—into the hands of her apostolic overseers—and as a result she was able to purchase her first home with a bankruptcy on her credit and no money down.

This is the power of honoring the Lord with your possessions and firstfruits as Proverbs 3:9-10 says, then connecting them to an apostolic anointing of deliverance, breakthrough, favor, and increase. Something amazing happens when money meets authority.

When targeting a grace or an anointing with a seed, make sure that you do not, and I repeat *do not*, base your decision solely upon what you see externally. There are many anointings or grace endowments that God has strategically hidden in this hour and will have to be perceived and spiritually discerned.

They don't have huge congregations and billions of dollars. They don't drive flashy cars or wear flashy suits. Now I'm not saying that people who have large congregations, billions of dollars, nice suits, and nice cars are not anointed. My husband and I have friends who pastor very large congregations, but these men and women of God are highly anointed and preach the Gospel for the right reasons, if you know what I mean. But we also have friends who have small congregations, and these people are walking in some power that would blow your mind!

Listen, I like nice suits and I wear nice suits. But the anointing or the grace that God has placed upon my life has nothing to do with what I am wearing. I can wear jeans, which I am known to wear even in my television appearances, a T-shirt, and a ball cap and still release that which God has placed in me and upon me. I don't need a big cross hanging around my neck to prove how anointed I am. So don't be led, governed, or dictated by these things. Be led by the Spirit of God.

If you are tired of struggling financially and going through the motions and not really experiencing all that God has for you, then get hold of this revelation. This revelation will not only change your finances; it will change your entire life. Give yourself first to God and then begin to ask Him to show you where to target the money and possessions that He has entrusted into your hands. As He reveals His divine intelligence to you, obey and stay connected to that anointing.

Over the years, I've seen where good people started out in this principle but later broke the connection. They started out flowing in amazing supernatural results through connecting themselves, their possessions, and money to an anointing. But when they broke the connection, the miracle flow stopped immediately. In a short matter of time these individuals returned to the place that God had delivered them from.

Another point I would like to make is this. As you begin to flow in this realm of supernatural abundance, please remember not to forsake your pastor and the house where you are being spiritually fed. Many times we will send financial seeds to other ministers and forget to bless the man and woman of God who are praying for us and feeding us faithfully each week. Don't make this mistake. Honor your leadership first. Send them on vacations, take them shopping, and help them pay off debts. When you do this, you are relieving them from earthly weights that hinder them from ministering at their fullest potential.

Once you have taken care of your own house, then pray about where to send additional offerings. For example, if this book has ministered to you and you sense a connection and a desire to sow financially into this supernatural grace, then do so. Just make sure that your own pastor, first lady, and the church you attend are being well taken care of first.

I said earlier that this revelation will change your life. So decide today to no longer be an unwise investor. Take your life, possessions, and money and target a grace gift and reap phenomenal results. Remember, when money meets apostolic authority, something explosive, amazing, and supernatural transpires.

Chapter 23

Holes and Back Doors

Ye have sown much, and bring in little; ye eat, but ye have not enough; ye drink, but ye are not filled with drink; ye clothe you, but there is none warm; and he that earneth wages earneth wages to put it into a bag with holes (Haggai 1:6).

Many people do not realize that there are doors in the spirit realm as there are in the natural realm. I didn't realize this until the Lord spoke to me one day and said, "Close the back door." I pondered what He had said, then I sensed a leading to get a sheet of paper and a pen.

I took the pen and began writing a list of names and events down on the sheet of paper. I noticed that all the names and events were intricately connected.

As I continued backtracking I could clearly see how the enemy had found an entrance into my life. It was so clear to me. Due to not paying what I had owed, promised, and vowed, the enemy had a legal right to create problems in my life. This is why many of the doors that my husband and I would walk through wouldn't last. I'm not saying this was the only problem, but it was sure something the Holy Spirit wanted us to learn so that we could teach others.

For example, God blesses you with a house. You're excited and praising God. But you forgot you didn't fulfill your financial obligation at the last house. Well, the enemy knows this and remembers this. So he waits until everything is going great for you in your new house, then all of a sudden things begin to go haywire. What happened? Here's what happened. There is a hole that hasn't been sealed and a door that hasn't been shut. When you walked away from the last house issue, how did you walk away? Now, there could be other dynamics around this issue, but for people who struggle to keep things and always find themselves losing properties, cars, and material things, this is definitely an area to check.

When you make a vow to God, your God, don't put off keeping it; God, your God, expects you to keep it and if you don't you're guilty. But if you don't make a vow in the first place, there's no sin. If you say

*you're going to do something, do it. Keep the vow
you willingly vowed to God, your God. You promised it, so do it* (Deuteronomy 23:21-23 MSG).

This Scripture is clearly telling us to do what we
say we're going to do; pay the debts that we owe and
fulfill our vows.

This is why you do not want to be presumptuous
in your giving. Many times our Christian telethons
are running and the anointing is flowing and we find
ourselves making commitments to these ministries;
but then when it's time to pay up, we do not fulfill
our part. These types of actions will create holes in
your life and cause all sorts of attacks to come about—
simply because of the vow or promise you made and
didn't keep.

So how do you seal up these holes and close the
back door? First you repent with all your heart. When
the Holy Spirit showed me this, I cried for days. I realized at that moment that I had not kept my word, and
in the realm of the spirit these things were being used
against me. I was deeply sorrowful, and God knew
it and extended His grace and mercy toward me. I
immediately saw a change in my life. It was like one
minute everything was dark and the next the sun was
shining brightly.

Although I repented and confessed this to the
Lord, I still had to fulfill my obligations. I knew I

didn't have all the money right then to pay everyone I owed. So I called on the help of the Holy Spirit. He told me to start right where I was, using what I had. See, people have more respect for you when you at least make an attempt to pay them. But when you just downright refuse to pay them or fulfill the obligation, they will have no respect for you.

So start where you are. Prioritize all the names of the people, creditors, or ministries you owe and start sending them what you can. As you step into this flow, God will begin to send additional funds to help you. In this way you're establishing character and sealing up spiritual holes and closing up spiritual doors. Also remember to seek the help and guidance of the Holy Spirit. He will show you clearly who and what you need to take care of.

One last thing I would like to say about holes and back doors is this. If you left your last church the wrong way, go and get it right. Once again, the spirit realm has this recorded. And it is one of the reasons you continue to church hop. I'm sure you would like to stop moving from church to church. In order to do this, simply, in the right attitude and under the leading and guidance of the Holy Spirit, make things right by repenting and confessing your faults. Don't spend a lot of time talking about what they did or didn't do. This is about you and your life success.

After you've done this, see how the Holy Spirit would have you approach the matter. He may have you call the pastor and ask for forgiveness. He may have you write a letter. Whatever He tells you, just do it. By doing this you are displaying godly character and integrity. You will be shutting the door to the enemy and cutting off his access into your life.

Contact Information for Lynetta Dent

Mailing Address:
PO Box 821, Cordova, TN 38088

Email: apostlelea@yahoo.com
Website: www.TheSiloamConnection.org

Other Books by Lynetta Dent

Sent

When a Prophet Prays...
Amazing Things Happen

Money Is Easy to Manifest

IN THE RIGHT HANDS, THIS BOOK WILL CHANGE LIVES!

Most of the people who need this message will not be looking for this book. To change their lives, you need to put a copy of this book in their hands.

> *But others (seeds) fell into good ground, and brought forth fruit, some a hundred-fold, some sixty-fold, some thirty-fold* (Matthew 13:8).

Our ministry is constantly seeking methods to find the good ground, the people who need this anointed message to change their lives. Will you help us reach these people?

> *Remember this—a farmer who plants only a few seeds will get a small crop. But the one who plants generously will get a generous crop* (2 Corinthians 9:6).

EXTEND THIS MINISTRY BY SOWING
3 BOOKS, 5 BOOKS, 10 BOOKS, **OR MORE TODAY,**
AND BECOME A LIFE CHANGER!

Thank you,

Don Nori Sr., Publisher
Destiny Image
Since 1982

DESTINY IMAGE PUBLISHERS, INC.

"Speaking to the Purposes of God for This Generation and for the Generations to Come."

VISIT OUR NEW SITE HOME AT
WWW.DESTINYIMAGE.COM

FREE SUBSCRIPTION TO DI NEWSLETTER

Receive free unpublished articles by top DI authors, exclusive

discounts, and free downloads from our best and newest books.

Visit www.destinyimage.com to subscribe.

Write to: Destiny Image
                P.O. Box 310
                Shippensburg, PA 17257-0310

Call: 1-800-722-6774

Email: orders@destinyimage.com

For a complete list of our titles or to place an order
online, visit www.destinyimage.com.